KU-222-111

Contents

THE NEW
Prepare for IELTS
ACADEMIC MODULES

Penny Cameron & Vanessa Todd

5 complete practice tests for Listening, Reading, Writing and Speaking in the test of the International English Language Testing System

UNIVERSITY OF TECHNOLOGY SYDNEY

INSEARCH

Insearch UTS and
International Programs,
University of Technology, Sydney

Insearch UTS
University of Technology, Sydney
Level 3, 187 Thomas Street
Sydney NSW 2000
Australia

International Programs
University of Technology, Sydney
Broadway NSW 2007
Australia

Produced by the Publications Department of Insearch Education
University of Technology, Sydney

The publisher would like to thank Mary Jane Hogan for her contribution
to the earlier editions of this book.

National Library of Australia
Cataloguing-in-Publication data

Cameron, Penny
The New Prepare for IELTS
Academic Modules

ISBN 0 908537 18 2

1. International English Language Testing System
2. English language - Examinations, questions, etc
3. English language - Textbooks for foreign speakers
I.   Cameron, Penny
II. Insearch UTS
III. University of Technology, Sydney. International Programs.
IV. Title V Title: The New Prepare for International English Language Testing System
VI. Title: Prepare for IELTS

Cover and layout by Simon Leong Design, Sydney.
Illustrations by Pam Horsnell, pp. 21, 22, 23, 37, 43, 103. All other diagrams by Simon Leong.
Printed by Southwood Press Pty Ltd, 76-82 Chapel Street Marrickville NSW Australia.

Unit 1
Introduction to the IELTS test

Part 1: About the IELTS test

Not only has English become an international language, it is used by more and more people around the world as a medium of post-school study. To help universities and colleges select students with sufficient English skills to succeed in their courses, the IELTS test was introduced in 1989 to assess "whether candidates are ready to study or train in the medium of English". It is now used for this purpose around the globe.

Depending on the course of study that students plan to take, students must elect to sit either the Academic IELTS test or the General Training IELTS test. This choice must be made when applying to sit the test. The Academic IELTS test is necessary for students who plan to study at university (undergraduate or postgraduate courses), and will test the student's ability both to understand and to use complex academic language. The General Training IELTS test is required by other institutions, such as colleges and high schools, for courses that require less complex language skills, and is also used as a general test of English proficiency e.g. for immigration purposes in Australia and New Zealand.

The Test Format

There are four subtests, or modules, to the IELTS test: Reading, Writing, Listening and Speaking. Students must sit all four subtests. While all students take the same Listening and Speaking tests, they sit different Reading and Writing tests, depending on whether they have selected the Academic IELTS test or the General Training IELTS test.

On the day of the test, the four subsections will be taken in the following order:

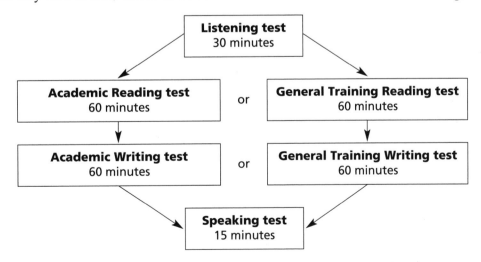

The Speaking test may even take place a day or two later at some test centres.

The Listening test lasts for about 30 minutes. It consists of four sections, played on cassette tape, in order of increasing difficulty. Each section might be a dialogue or a monologue. The test is played once only, and the questions for each section must be answered while listening, although time is given for students to check their answers. **Unit 2** of this book contains five practice Listening tests, recorded on the accompanying cassette tape.

The Reading test lasts for 60 minutes. Students are given either an Academic Reading test, or a General Training Reading test. Both tests consist of three sections, and in both tests different question types are used to assess students' comprehension. In both tests the sections are in order of increasing difficulty. **Unit 3** of this book contains five Reading practice tests.

The Writing test also lasts for 60 minutes. Again, students take either an Academic test, or a General Training test. Students must perform two writing tasks, which require different styles of writing. There is no choice of question topics. For more detail and Writing practice tests, turn to **Unit 4** of this book.

The Speaking test consists of a one-to-one interview with a specially trained examiner. The examiner will lead the candidate through the three parts of the test: an introduction and interview, an individual long turn where the candidate speaks for one to two minutes on a particular topic, and a two-way discussion thematically linked to the individual long turn. This interview will last for approximately 11-14 minutes. For more detail, turn to **Unit 5** of this book.

How the test is marked

Each module is marked on a scale from 1 up to 9. These bands are given according to highly detailed marking guidelines. These marking guidelines are not made public, but correspond roughly to the following descriptions:

1. Non User
2. Intermittent User
3. Extremely Limited User
4. Limited User
5. Modest User
6. Competent User
7. Good User
8. Very Good User
9. Expert User

The test results form will show the mark for each module as well as an average (overall) band score.

What do the band scores mean?

There is no pass or fail mark in the IELTS test. The marks, or bands, that a student receives show their ability to use and understand English. However, it is up to each university and college to decide what bands will be acceptable for entry into each course. This will usually depend on the language requirements for the course, that is, how difficult is the level of language that students are required to use and understand in each course.

The advantages of the IELTS test

The IELTS test is very comprehensive. It rates a student's ability to use English in the four major language skill areas: Reading, Writing, Listening and Speaking. Each module contains a variety of question types, and all of them are designed to simulate the language tasks that are needed in real life academic and training situations. Thus the scores that a student achieves in the IELTS test will give the student and the institution to which they have applied a clear idea of the student's ability to use English and whether their language skills are strong enough for them to study their desired course, or to fit more easily into the English-speaking community.

The interval between tests

Students may take the IELTS test as many times as they like, but after sitting an IELTS test, they must wait for THREE MONTHS before they can take it again. This is an official rule, but in any case it is unlikely that a student's score will improve in less than three months.

Part 2: For the student: How to prepare for IELTS

In this chapter you will find some suggestions for activities and approaches to help you do your best in the IELTS test. You will probably find it most useful after you have completed one or more of the practice tests in this book.

Analyse your weaknesses

To begin with, read the following statements and tick ☑ any that apply to you.

Listening	I cannot listen and read the questions at the same time **(E)**	☐
	I do not understand what the question is asking me to do **(E)**	☐
	I do not understand what I hear **(L)**	☐
Reading	I run out of time and do not answer all the questions **(F)**	☐
	It takes me a long time to read the passages **(E)**	☐
	I do not understand what the question is asking me to do **(E)**	☐
	I do not understand the reading passages **(L)**	☐
Writing	I am not sure what the question means **(E)**	☐
	I cannot write quickly enough **(E)**	☐
	I do not have enough ideas to write about on the topic **(L)**	☐
	I cannot say what I think in English **(L)**	☐
Speaking	I get nervous and make mistakes **(E)**	☐
	The examiner asks me questions I have not thought about before **(E)**	☐
	I do not understand the examiner's questions **(L)**	☐
	I feel threatened when the examiner asks me to speak for 1 or 2 minutes **(F)**	☐

After each statement you will find a letter: **F**, **E** or **L**. These refer to: **Format**, **Exam Practice** and **Language Practice**. As you read the sections below, you will find suggestions under each heading to help you improve your IELTS score.

Know the Format

An important preparation for the IELTS test is to find out about the structure of the test. What are the sections of the test? Which one comes first? Second? How much time is allowed for each section? How many questions are there? How long must I speak?

These are simple questions to answer, but important. Once you are familiar with the test format, you will be more relaxed. You will be able to focus on answering questions well, rather than worrying about how many questions there are, or how much time is left.

You will find the answers to these questions in the introduction to this book, and (in more detail) in the *IELTS Handbook*, available from test administration centres.

Exam Practice

Once you have found out about the format of the IELTS exam, you need to practise your **exam skills**. These are techniques to help you show off your language skills during the short time you have in the exam.

The first skill to work on is **timing**. You will have to practise reading and writing under time constraints. Practise speed reading every day. Try reading a short passage in a fixed time (for example, set yourself three minutes to read it quickly). You will not understand everything in the first reading, but you will become more used to skimming a text to get a general idea of its main points. Then you can come back to read certain parts of the text with more attention.

Likewise, try writing for a set period of time every day. For this exercise, total accuracy is not necessary; rather you are trying to practise getting your ideas down on paper quickly. Set yourself a different topic each day, such as Computers, the Family, Industry in my country, etc., and write as much as you can for, say, five minutes. Write notes to your friends, or short descriptions of something you have seen. Your speed will improve gradually, and will be very useful in the exam, when you must write a certain number of words for each task in a set period of time.

Another exam preparation is to familiarise yourself with the **question types** used in the IELTS exam. There are many different types, and they do not all appear in every exam. But by knowing some types, you will be familiar with the kinds of tasks you are expected to do, and you will save time because you can interpret the question more easily.

Start with the exams in this book. Do each test under exam conditions, then afterwards look at the tests again. What kind of questions were asked in each section? Multiple choice? Short answers? Matching parts of sentences? Filling in diagrams? Look at the kinds of questions used, and what they are asking you to do. If you had problems with any of them, do them again, slowly, so that you are sure of what you are doing. Then when you sit the real test, you will be more familiar with the kinds of questions asked, and will understand what you have to do more quickly.

Note: always read the questions carefully. Do not assume they will be exactly the same as the practice tests!

Finally, you might think about sitting a real IELTS test "just for practice". You will get to know how it works, and get practice working under exam conditions. Then, when you are ready to take the IELTS test in earnest, you will know about the IELTS format, and will have already practised your exam skills.

If this is not possible, you can ask other students who have taken the IELTS test about their experience, and find out which tasks they think require the most preparation.

Language Practice, in class and on your own

This is where the hard work lies. Exam practice and knowing the format will help you in the IELTS test by leaving you free to concentrate on your language skills. However, you will need to work hard to further develop these skills.

The IELTS test measures how well students can perform the language skills needed for study. To do this, it uses the kinds of tasks that might be found in real-life situations. Therefore, you will not be able to simply memorise answers. Your IELTS score will be a reflection of your language ability, and to do well, you will have to work on your language skills. To achieve the IELTS score you want will require hard work, usually with the help of a teacher.

Class Work

In class your teacher will be introducing and extending a range of skills, all essential for the IELTS test. These will include:

Speaking: pronunciation and intonation practice, fluency practice, using and understanding common phrases, interacting with other speakers, speaking for an extended time on a particular topic, discussing that topic.

Listening: recognising voice tone (questions, surprise, etc.), listening for keywords, listening for general information, listening for numbers, listening for discourse markers (*firstly, secondly, Or I could say that another way, the most significant result was that ...*).

Reading: skimming (to get a general understanding), scanning (looking for specific information), vocabulary development, summarising, determining the writer's attitude and opinion.

Writing: adjusting style according to purpose, writing paragraphs, introductions and conclusions, using conjunctions and reference, organising information within a text, using supporting evidence to prove a claim.

Make the most of the work you study in class by reviewing it regularly. Re-read your class notes; note carefully any areas where you had problems. Work on them again and see your teacher if you still have questions. Try to use new vocabulary in your writing compositions, or in conversation. Practise grammatical structures in the same way.

Your teacher knows what you need and will try to help you overcome language problems. By going over lessons you will get the maximum benefit from your teacher's skills and work.

Out of class work

Most experts agree that the quickest way to improve in a language is to immerse yourself in it. Therefore, to improve your English skills, try to get into as many situations where you and other people are using English.

This may be difficult if you live in a non-English speaking country. However, try to find English interest groups, go to English films and listen to English on the radio. Read English books and magazines.

In an English-speaking country this is much easier. Wherever there are people, you will be able to use and understand English. English books and magazines will also be easier to obtain. Try to spend as much of your day as possible using English. You will probably end up dreaming in English, too!

A final word

The practice tests in this book are designed to help you understand the nature of the test. You cannot use your results in these tests to accurately predict your performance in a live IELTS test where you will be doing an examination with all its attendant stresses. You can, however, get to know the form of the test very well.

With all this preparation - getting to know the format of the IELTS test, practising exam techniques, class work and private study - you will be ready to do your best in the IELTS exam.

Try also to relax, and do some activities that you enjoy. An occasional break from your studies will give you fresh energy and motivation to continue studying hard.

The day of the test

After all your preparation for the IELTS test, follow these simple suggestions to ensure your test day goes smoothly.

- Plan to arrive early (perhaps half an hour). Then if you have unexpected transport problems or some other delay, you will have extra time to sort them out before the test starts. There is nothing worse than arriving late, upset and flustered, when you need all your mental energy for the exam.

- Don't worry about the parts of the test that are finished, or those yet to come. Concentrate fully on the module you have in front of you.

- Use your time carefully. Don't spend too much time on any one answer; if you do, you may not answer the other questions properly. Don't finish quickly, then sit doing nothing. In the time remaining, check your answers - you might change a wrong answer to a right answer and gain extra marks.

The Listening test

- Before each listening section is played, read the questions through quickly. The vocabulary (and any diagrams) will give you some idea of what you are about to hear.

- Note what kinds of questions you must answer: filling in numbers, choosing a description, finding the speaker's opinion. You will then make the most of what you hear, because you will know what to listen for.

The Reading test

- You have one hour to answer questions on three sections, so divide up your time - perhaps 15 minutes for the first section, 20 minutes for the second section, and 25 minutes for the third section (the sections get harder as you go on, so you might like to spend more time on the last one).

- As a general strategy, do not start by reading the passage. You do not yet know what information you are looking for, and you will waste precious time if you try to read and understand everything.

  Firstly, read the heading of the text. This will give you a very general idea of what the passage is about.

  Secondly, quickly read through the questions. How many questions are there relating to this text? What kind of questions are they? (sentence completion, diagram completion ...). This will help you focus when you read the text, as you will have some idea what to look for.

  Thirdly, turn to the reading passage, and read it through quickly. The purpose here is to get a general understanding of the passage - you do not need to understand every detail.

Finally, turn again to the questions and begin to work through them, referring back to the passage when you need to, and reading important sections carefully and slowly.

If at any time you cannot answer a question, or it is taking you a long time, leave it and come back to it at the end.

The Writing test

The style and shape of your answer will be covered in more detail in **Unit 4** of this book.

On a very practical level, however:

- write in pen (not pencil), as it is easier to read. Bring several pens to the test with you.

- do not write a rough draft, then re-write it. You will waste valuable time.

- use time at the end to check for small errors: verb agreements, plurals, punctuation, verb tense. These things are easily corrected and affect what mark your work will receive.

The Speaking test

Preparation for this test will be covered in more detail in **Unit 5** of this book.

Some things to think about:

- Talk to your friends in English while you are waiting for your interview.

- Do not simply answer the examiner's questions; elaborate on your answers. Talk as much as possible. This is not rude; the examiner needs to hear you talk a lot, so he or she can find out your proficiency level.

- You will find it easier to talk if you have something to say. Use the suggestions in Unit 5 to prepare for the interview. Think about your opinions and your reasons for holding them. Think of important/funny/exciting things that have happened to you and be ready to talk about them.

- Phase 2 of the test requires you to speak for one to two minutes. Use all the information on the card to help you, and practise with a timer so you know how long you should speak.

If you prepare carefully for the IELTS test using the practice tests and the strategies in **Units 4** and **5**, and note the hints for the day of the test, you will show your language skills to their best advantage.

Good luck!

Unit 2
The Listening test

How to use this Unit

This Unit contains:

- A photocopiable master of a Listening Practice Tests Answer Sheet which resembles the actual Answer Sheet you will use in an IELTS test. Make a copy of this Answer Sheet to use for each Listening Practice Test.

- Five Listening Practice Tests. Each test, which is made up of four sections, should take 30 minutes only, plus 10 minutes to transfer your answers to the Answer Sheet, as you will do in the real IELTS test.

  Each Listening Practice Test is recorded on cassette. There is no need to stop the cassette during a test; all pauses for you to read the next questions are included on the cassette.

In Unit 1 of this book you will find general information about the Listening Module and strategies to help you before you begin.

You should complete each test under exam conditions. DO NOT use a dictionary to help you until after you have completed each Practice Test.

Write your answers on each page as you complete each question, as you would in an IELTS test. After you have finished each Listening Practice Test, transfer your answers to a Listening Practice Tests Answer Sheet before you correct them. This will give you practice in transferring your answers, which must be done with care.

The answers to each Listening Practice Test can be found in Unit 6, along with complete tapescripts for you to confirm your understanding of information and of vocabulary items.

Listening Practice Tests Answer Sheet

You may photocopy this page.

Transfer your answers from the question pages to this Answer Sheet at the end of the Listening Test.

Use one Answer Sheet for each Listening Practice Test.

1		22	
2		23	
3		24	
4		25	
5		26	
6		27	
7		28	
8		29	
9		30	
10		31	
11		32	
12		33	
13		34	
14		35	
15		36	
16		37	
17		38	
18		39	
19		40	
20		41	
21		42	

Listening total:

Listening Practice Test 1

SECTION 1 *Questions 1-12*

Questions 1-8

Listen to the conversation between a student, Angela Tung, and Bob Wills, who is the student adviser at a language school. Complete the form. **Write NO MORE THAN THREE WORDS OR NUMBERS for each answer.**

REQUEST FOR SPECIAL LEAVE

Name: _____*Angela Tung*_____

Example   Student number: _____*H 5712*_____

Address: **(1)** _____*Tamworth, 2340*

Telephone number: _____*810 6745*_____

Course: **(2)** _____

Teacher's name: **(3)** _____

Student visa expiry date: **(4)** _____

I wish to request leave in Term: **(5)** _____

Dates of leave: **(6)** _____ to   **(7)** _____

Number of working days missed: **(8)** _____

Questions 9-12

Circle the appropriate letter A-D.

9.   Why does Angela want to take leave?

      A   to visit her aunt and uncle
      B   to see the National Gallery
      C   to see the Southern Highlands
      D   to study more writing

10.   Where is Angela going?

      A   Tamworth
      B   Brisbane
      C   Armidale
      D   Sydney

11.   Who is going with Angela?

      A   her uncle
      B   her mother
      C   her aunt
      D   her father

12.   When will Angela go home to her own country?

      A   in five years
      B   in twelve months
      C   in two months
      D   when her mother goes home

SECTION 2   *Questions 13-24*

Questions 13-18

Complete the calendar while you listen to the tape. Use words from the box. There are more words in the box than you need. Some words may be used more than once.

cleaner	garbage	filters	stove
dry cleaner	charity	gardener	paper
lift	library	electricity	water

Sunday	Monday	Tuesday	Wednesday	Thursday	Friday	Saturday
May 17	18	19 (16) ____	20	21	22 (13) ____	23
24	25 (17) ____	26	27	28	29 (14) ____	30
31 (18) ____	**June** 1	2	3	4	5 (15) ____	6

Questions 19-24

Circle the appropriate letter A-D.

19. Where has Martha gone?

   A London
   B Sydney
   C New York
   D Paris

20. Why is Martha away from home?

   A She's visiting friends
   B She's at a conference
   C She's on business
   D She's setting up a business

21. Who will Martha meet while she's away?

   A an old school friend
   B a friend of her mother's
   C an old university friend
   D an old teacher

22. What has Martha left for John?

   A a letter
   B a meal
   C a book
   D a bill

23. Who does Martha want John to telephone?

   A the optometrist
   B the telephone company
   C the doctor
   D the dentist

24. What is the code for Martha's alarm system?

   A enter 2190
   B 2190 enter
   C 9120 enter
   D enter 9120

SECTION 3   *Questions 25-36*

Questions 25-29

Complete the table below. Write **NO MORE THAN THREE WORDS OR NUMBERS**
for each answer.

LANGUAGE SCHOOL ENROLMENT FORM

Name of Applicant: *Vijay Paresh*

Telephone number: *909 2467*

Language to be learned: **(25)** _____

Location of class: **(26)** _____

Time of class: **(27)** _____

Name of class: **(28)** _____

Date of commencement of class: **(29)** _____

Questions 30-32

*Circle the appropriate letters **A-D**.*

30. Anne is

    A   Vijay's friend
    B   Denise's friend
    C   Vijay's boss
    D   Denise's boss.

31. When Anne speaks she

    A   congratulates Denise
    B   ignores Denise
    C   criticises Denise
    D   praises Denise.

32. When Denise replies she

    A   laughs at Anne
    B   sympathises with Anne
    C   argues with Anne
    D   apologises to Anne.

Questions 33-36

Listen to the directions and match the places in questions 33-36 to the appropriate letter A-H on the plan.

33. Reception area, admissions _____

34. Fees office _____

35. Book and stationery supply _____

36. Travel agency _____

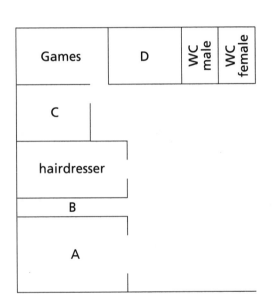
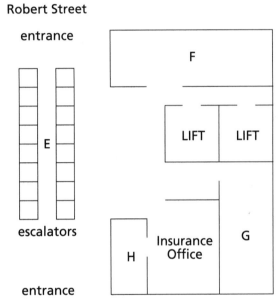

SECTION 4   *Questions 37-41*

Questions 37-38

Look at questions 37-38 below and study the grid. Tick all the relevant boxes in each column.

CITY	37. Cities with old-structure problems	38. Cities with good public transport
Los Angeles		
London		
Bangkok		
Hong Kong		
New York		
Taipei		
Houston		
Sydney		
Paris		
Tokyo		
Dallas		

Questions 39-41

*Write **NO MORE THAN THREE WORDS** to complete these sentences.*

39.   The public transport available in Houston is   _____

40.   To reduce peak hour traffic jams, people can travel   _____

41.   Vehicles carrying more than one passenger can use   _____

Listening Practice Test 2

SECTION 1   Questions 1-10

Questions 1-4

Listen to the conversation between two people in a shop which sells electronic goods. Put a circle around the letter of the item they choose.

Example:

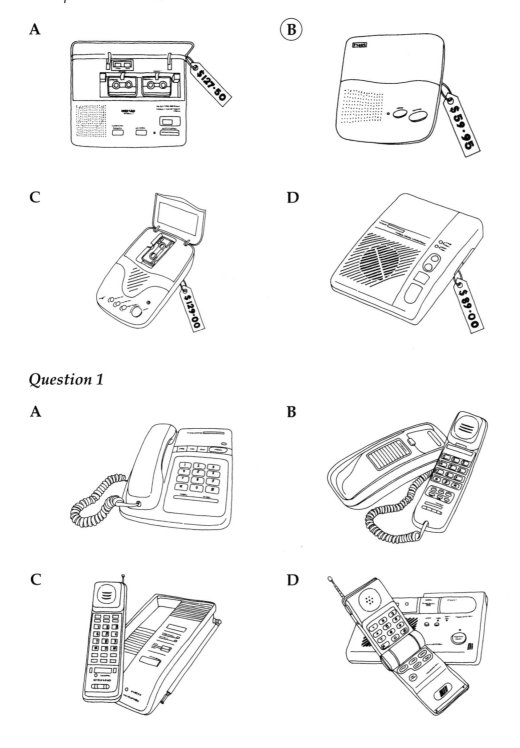

A

B

C

D

Question 1

A

B

C

D

Question 2

A

B

C
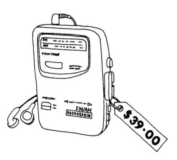

D

Question 3

A

B

C

D

THE NEW PREPARE FOR IELTS: Academic Modules
Unit 2 The Listening test

Question 4

A

B

C

D

Questions 5-10

Write **NO MORE THAN THREE WORDS** *for each answer.*

5. Where will Mary go now? _____

6. Who is waiting for Tom? _____

7. What time does Mary expect to come home? _____

8. Where is Mary's office? _____

9. What TV program does Tom plan to watch tonight? _____

10. Where does Tom have to go tomorrow? _____

SECTION 2   Questions 11-22

Questions 11-17

Complete the request to terminate or transfer form.

REQUEST TO TERMINATE OR TRANSFER CLASSES

Message for: **(11)** _____ Student affairs

Student's family name: **(12)** _____

Student's first name: **(13)** _____

Student number: **(14)** _____

Teacher's name: **(15)** _____

Student's address: **(16)** _____

                        (11) _____

Telephone: **(17)** _____

Questions 18-22

Circle the appropriate letter A-D.

18.   May wants to change classes because

    A   she doesn't like her teacher
    B   too many students share a language
    C   she can't understand the work
    D   the class is too large.

19.   In the evening class most students' first language is

    A   English
    B   Italian
    C   Spanish
    D   Japanese.

20.   There is room in the new class because two students

    A   went home
    B   dropped the course
    C   transferred
    D   graduated.

21.   May prefers the evening class because it is

    A   in the same room
    B   in the room next door
    C   in the same building
    D   in the building next door.

22.   May wants Mrs Brooks to leave a message at

    A   the library
    B   her work
    C   her friend's house
    D   her home.

SECTION 3   *Questions 23-31*

Questions 23-27

Complete the table showing the students' opinions. Choose your answers from the box below. There are more words than spaces so you will not use them all. You may use any of the words more than once.

INSTRUMENT

guitar	violin	pipa
organ	flute	bouzouki
piano	drums	harp

STYLE OF MUSIC

ballet music	rap	classical
heavy metal	opera	jazz
rock	be-bop	country

Student	favourite instrument	favourite style of music
Example **Greg**	*drums*	*classical*
(23) **Alexandria**		
(24) **Katja**		
(25) **Rachel**		
(26) **Harry**		
(27) **Emiko**		

Questions 28-31

Write **NO MORE THAN THREE WORDS** to complete the sentences.

28. Stimulating music speeds up our _____

29. Calming music reduces our _____

30. _____ music has very predictable rhythms.

31. Research may show if people of different _____ perceive music differently.

SECTION 4   *Questions 32-40*

Questions 32-36

Using **NO MORE THAN THREE WORDS**, *answer the following questions.*

32.   Who should take charge of the patient's health?

_____

33.   What, in the speaker's opinion, is the single greatest threat to health?

_____

34.   Which group in the study was most at risk of early death?

_____

35.   Which environmental hazard does the speaker find most under-rated?

_____

36.   What will be improved by an education campaign?

_____

Questions 37-40

Write **NO MORE THAN THREE WORDS** *to complete the sentences.*

37.   Statistics quoted show that _____ would prevent many illnesses.

38.   Exercise should be _____ , so find someone to join you in your activity.

39.   One important way of preventing sports injury is by adequate _____

40.   Injuries can also be reduced by using _____ techniques.

Listening Practice Test 3

SECTION 1   *Questions 1-8*

Questions 1-5

Listen to the conversation between the manager of the Student Hostel and a student. Tick (✓) if the information is correct, or write in the changes.

STUDENT HOSTEL

Charges for meals

Example

BREAKFAST	$2.00	*$2.50*
LUNCH	$3.00	✓

DINNER	$3.00	**(1)**	_____
THREE MEAL PLAN	$48.00 per week	**(2)**	_____
TWO MEAL PLAN	$36.00 per week	**(3)**	_____

Meal Times

BREAKFAST	7.00 - 9.30 am	**(4)**	_____
LUNCH	noon - 2.00 pm		
DINNER	6.00 -7.30 pm	**(5)**	_____

Questions 6-8

Listen to the conversation and match the places in questions 6-8 to the appropriate letters *A-F* on the map.

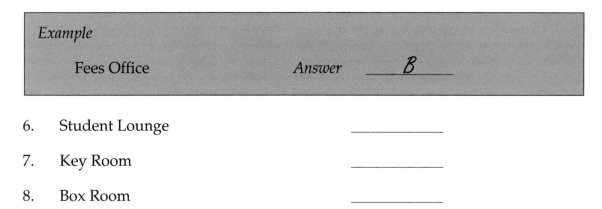

Example

Fees Office   *Answer*   _____*B*_____

6.   Student Lounge   _____

7.   Key Room   _____

8.   Box Room   _____

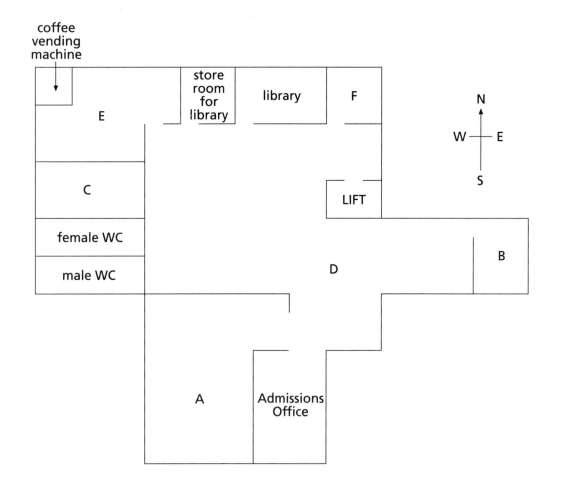

SECTION 2   *Questions 9-19*

Questions 9-16

Listen while a teacher tells you how to complete this note. Write NO MORE THAN THREE WORDS OR NUMBERS for each answer.

SCHOOL EXCURSION PERMISSION NOTE

Example

    Class: *3A*

School excursion to: **(9)** _____

on: **(10)** _____
               day   *date*

Bus will depart from: **(11)** _____   at: **(12)** _____

Bus will return to: **(13)** _____   at: **(14)** _____

Students must bring: **(15)** _____

Clothing: students will need: **(16)** _____

_____
Signature of Guardian / Group Leader

Questions 17-19

Write NO MORE THAN THREE WORDS OR NUMBERS for each answer.

17. When will the bus get to the Blue Mountains?   _____

18. What special equipment is on the bus?   _____

19. What other class is going on the excursion?   _____

SECTION 3   *Questions 20-30*

Questions 20-22

Complete the table which shows when visitors may go to the different parts of the hospital.

	Intensive Care	Maternity	Surgical	Emergency
Permitted visiting hours	*Example* *6 am – midnight*	**(20)**	**(21)**	**(22)**

Questions 23-25

Complete the table showing who is allowed to visit, and the number of visitors permitted.

A	=	Adults may visit
E	=	Everyone may visit
I	=	Immediate family only

	Intensive Care	Maternity	Surgical	Emergency
Visitors permitted	*Example* *I* *2*	**(23)**	**(24)**	**(25)**

Questions 26-27

*Circle **TWO** letters.*

Example	On Monday Andrew will visit these wards
	Ⓐ male surgical
	Ⓑ female surgical
	C children's surgical
	D male geriatric
	E female geriatric
	F infectious diseases.

26.   On Tuesday Andrew will be with

   A   Dr Chang
   B   Dr Thomas
   C   Dr Gray
   D   Dr Robertson
   E   Dr Shay
   F   Dr Kominski.

27.   On Thursday and Friday Andrew will visit

   A   the nursery
   B   the hospital gymnasium
   C   the administration office
   D   the school room
   E   the teenage ward
   F   the children's ward.

Questions 28-30

*Write **NO MORE THAN THREE WORDS OR NUMBERS** for each answer.*

28.   What time on Wednesday morning will Andrew be in lectures?

   _____

29 .   How many first year students are there?

   _____

30.   What job does Andrew's father do?

   _____

SECTION 4   *Questions 31-38*

Questions 31-35

Write **NO MORE THAN THREE WORDS** *to complete these sentences.*

31.   Samuel Wells _____ before Scholastic House opened in 1903.

32.   Scholastic House became _____ in 1963.

33.   There were _____ original students.

34.   One of these students became a prominent _____ .

35.   The college has a tradition of learning and _____ .

Questions 36-38

Circle the appropriate letter A-D.

36.   The college discusses controversial issues because it

    A   informs the debate
    B   reduces tension
    C   encourages argument
    D   brings positive publicity.

37.   The principal believes that

    A   science is less advanced than medicine
    B   philosophy is more useful than science
    C   science is ahead of philosophy
    D   science is more useful than philosophy.

38.   The principal urges the students to

    A   accept what they are told
    B   ask questions at all times
    C   think only about their studies
    D   think where progress will lead them.

Listening Practice Test 4

SECTION 1   Questions 1-8

*Listen to the conversation and complete the table. Write **C** for Cookery, **S** for Sports and **T** for Travel.*

Name of author	C = Cookery S = Sports T = Travel
Peter Adams	*Example* ST
Stephen Bau	**(1)**
Pam Campbell	**(2)**
C. Kezik	S
Ari Hussein	**(3)**
Sally Innes	S
Meg Jorgensen	**(4)**
Bruno Murray	**(5)**
Ruby Lee	**(6)**
Jim Wells	**(7)**
Helen Yeung	**(8)**

SECTION 2   *Questions 9-18*

Questions 9-14

Look at this invitation. Tick (✓) if the information is correct or write in the changes.

Example	Answer
INVITATION TO A WELCOMING LUNCH	*dance party*
AT BLACKWELL HOUSE	✓
ON FRIDAY JUNE 15 AT 8 PM	**(9)** _____
THE PARTY WILL END AT 10 PM	**(10)** _____
FREE TRANSPORT TO THE STUDENT HOSTEL IS AVAILABLE LEAVING BLACKWELL HOUSE AT 10.30	**(11)** _____
OTHER STUDENTS MAY ATTEND	**(12)** _____
PLEASE BRING YOUR STUDENT IDENTIFICATION CARD	**(13)** _____
PLEASE REPLY BY TUESDAY IF YOU CAN COME	**(14)** _____

Questions 15-18

*Complete the sentences below. Write **NO MORE THAN THREE WORDS** for each answer.*

15. There is new road work on

_____

16. Do not use Blackwell Street because workmen are

_____

17. When you pass the roundabout, go along Brown Crescent into

_____

18. It's wise to use the

_____

SECTION 3   Questions 19-29

Questions 19-23

Label the parts of the lawn sprinkler. Choose words from the box below. There are more words in the box than you will need.

Write the appropriate words on the diagram.

holes	base	crank
spray tube	handle	gears
hinge	hose pipe	water wheel
guide	chain guard	pulley

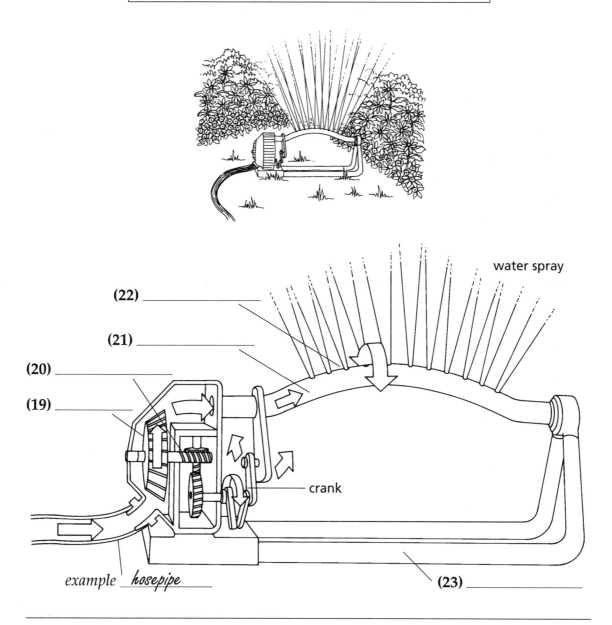

(22) _____

(21) _____

(20) _____

(19) _____

water spray

crank

example *hosepipe*

(23) _____

Questions 24-29

Circle the appropriate letter A-D.

24. The last examinations will be held on

    A   November 26
    B   November 29
    C   December 2
    D   December 4.

25. Scott is going to the United States

    A   to study
    B   to teach
    C   to travel
    D   to visit friends.

26. The general science course in the United States is

    A   similar
    B   simple
    C   difficult
    D   different.

27. Linda has had an extension to

    A   complete her assignment
    B   do more research
    C   study
    D   go on holiday.

28. Communications and English will be examined on

    A   December 1 morning
    B   December 2 morning
    C   December 1 afternoon
    D   December 2 afternoon.

29. Mark finds teaching this class

    A   boring
    B   tiring
    C   depressing
    D   stimulating.

SECTION 4   *Questions 30-39*

Questions 30-39

Complete the summary. Use words from the box. There are more words in the box than you need. Some words may be used more than once.

rest	relaxed	angry	warm
stress	work	hunger	45 degrees
chew	exhaustion	desk	40 degrees
noise	tense	study	crowded
speak	smoky	relaxation	
tired	exercise	raised	

The most usual cause of headaches is **(30)** _____. Headaches can also come as a result of excessive **(31)** _____.

Some people say they get a headache when they **(32)** _____. This is probably because they get very **(33)** _____.

It may also be because they are working in poor light which makes them very **(34)** _____. It is helpful if your reading material is on a bookrest at **(35)** _____ to the desk. It is also important to be **(36)** _____ in bed.

You may even get a headache because you **(37)** _____ too hard.

The best advice is to try to eat regular meals, get enough **(38)** _____ and avoid **(39)** _____ places.

Listening Practice Test 5

SECTION 1   *Questions 1-9*

Questions 1-7

Listen to the conversation between Megan and Ken about how they will spend the evening. Circle the appropriate letter.

> *Example:* What is Thomas's new home phone number?
>
> A   9731 4322   B   9813 4562   Ⓒ   9452 3456   D   9340 2367

1.   What will Ken and Megan do this evening?

    A    **B**   **C**   **D**

2.   Where is Entertainment City?

    A    **B**

    C    **D**

3.   When will Ken leave?

  A   now
  B   in ten minutes' time
  C   at 10 o'clock
  D   in 30 minutes

4.   How will Megan travel to Entertainment City?

  A   **B**   **C**   **D**

  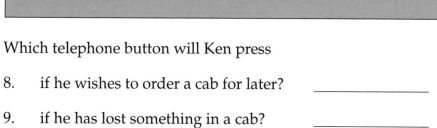

5.   How many people will they meet there?

  A   none
  B   three
  C   two
  D   a group

6.   How much will the evening cost?

  A   nothing
  B   just the fares
  C   less than $40.00
  D   more than $40.00

7.   What time does Megan plan to come home?

  A   before midnight
  B   after midnight
  C   on the last bus
  D   on the last train

Questions 8-9

*Write **ONE NUMBER** for each answer.*

Which telephone button will Ken press:

Example: If he wishes to order a cab now?	*1*

Which telephone button will Ken press

8.   if he wishes to order a cab for later?   _____

9.   if he has lost something in a cab?   _____

SECTION 2   Questions 10-20

Questions 10-15

Complete the notes below. Write **NO MORE THAN THREE WORDS OR NUMBERS**
for each answer in the spaces provided.

The plane will leave Gatwick Airport at **(10)** _____ in the morning. The

transport from Athens Airport will be by **(11)** _____ . The hotel is booked

for **(12)** _____ nights. During our stay, the group will visit the National

Archaeological Museum in the morning. Group members will then have free time on

(13) _____ evening. The group will see the Greek Islands and will travel

by **(14)** _____ . Traditional **(15)** _____ will be part of the package.

Questions 16-18

Circle **TWO** *letters*

16. The organiser would like to thank

    A   the Greek government
    B   the travel agent
    C   British Airways
    D   staff at the British Museum.

17. People should bring to the party

    A   photographs
    B   food
    C   camera
    D   drinks.

18. The members of the group share an interest in

    A   Greek culture
    B   studying old societies
    C   fine food
    D   travel.

Questions 19-20

Complete this baggage label.
Write **NO MORE THAN THREE**
WORDS *in the spaces provided.*

19 _____

20 _____

SECTION 3   Questions 21-31

Questions 21-26

*Write **NO MORE THAN THREE WORDS OR NUMBERS** for each answer.*

21.   When did the Language Learning Centre enter its new building? _____

22.   Which country do most of the students come from now? _____

23.   What were the Indonesians studying at the Language Learning Centre?

_____

24.   How long should students stay at the Language Learning Centre?

_____

25.   What is the most common class size? _____

26.   Who does Dr Robinson consider to be the best promoters of the Centre?

_____

Questions 27-31

Complete the table showing which activities are available. Tick (✓) in the column if an activity is available.

Activity	all students	beginners	advanced students
Example **Soccer club**	✓		
(27) Non-English language courses			
(28) Jazz club			
(29) Drama society			
(30) Choral group			
(31) Special conversation group			

SECTION 4   *Questions 32-40*

Questions 32-37

Circle the appropriate letter A-D

32. Most postgraduate students are studying

    A courses that feature vocational training
    B full-time courses
    C part-time courses
    D research-based courses.

33. Postgraduate students are advised to

    A take as many diverse subjects as possible
    B accept an intellectual challenge
    C be sure to have a definite goal
    D have already completed training.

34. The speaker says that where you study

    A is of minimal importance
    B must be somewhere you like
    C must be reasonably priced
    D should be based on your course.

35. Choosing an institution should be mainly based on

    A the quality of the housing for postgraduate students
    B the reputation of the department they work in
    C the reputation of the organisation they attend
    D the quality of the supervision they receive.

36. These facilities are the most important to the speaker:

    A libraries and laboratories
    B computer facilities
    C secretarial support
    D recreational organisations.

37. Postgraduates can avoid feeling alone by

    A joining associations of their peers
    B developing outside interests
    C participating in the outside community
    D making friends outside the university.

Questions 38-40

Complete the sentences below. Write **NO MORE THAN THREE WORDS** *for each answer.*

38.   Students should not forget to budget for their

_____

39.   Students should check all study costs carefully because institutions may

_____

40.   Postgraduate students cannot get loans from

_____

Unit 3
The Reading test

How to use this Unit

This Unit contains:

- A photocopiable master of a Reading Practice Tests Answer Sheet which resembles the actual Answer Sheet you will use in an IELTS test. Make a copy of this Answer Sheet to use for each Reading Practice Test.

- Five Academic Reading Practice Tests. Each test, which is made up of three sections, should take one hour.

In Unit 1 of this book you will find general information about the Reading Module and strategies to help you before you begin.

You should complete each test under exam conditions. DO NOT use a dictionary to help you until after you have completed each Practice Test.

Write your answers on a copy of the Reading Practice Tests Answer Sheet (see the next page). Do not write your answers on the question pages, because in an IELTS test all answers in the Reading test are written on an Answer Sheet.

The answers to each Academic Reading Practice Test can be found in Unit 6.

Reading Practice Tests Answer Sheet

You may photocopy this page.

Use one Answer Sheet for each Reading Practice Test.

1		**22**	
2		**23**	
3		**24**	
4		**25**	
5		**26**	
6		**27**	
7		**28**	
8		**29**	
9		**30**	
10		**31**	
11		**32**	
12		**33**	
13		**34**	
14		**35**	
15		**36**	
16		**37**	
17		**38**	
18		**39**	
19		**40**	
20		**41**	
21		**42**	

Reading total:

THE NEW PREPARE FOR IELTS: Academic Modules
Unit 3 The Reading test

Academic Reading Practice Test 1

Reading Passage 1

You should spend about 20 minutes on Questions 1-13 which are based on Reading Passage 1.

Airconditioning the Earth

The circulation of air in the atmosphere is activated by convection, the transference of heat resulting from the fact that warm gases or fluids rise while cold gases or fluids sink. For example: if one wall of a room is heated whilst the opposite wall is cooled, air will rise against the warm wall and flow across the ceiling to the cold wall before descending to flow back across the floor to the warm wall again.

The real atmosphere, however, is like a very long room with a very low ceiling. The distance from equator to pole is 10,000 km., while the "ceiling height" to the beginning of the stratosphere is only about 10 km. The air therefore splits up into a number of smaller loops or convection cells. Between the equator and each pole there are three such cells and within these the circulation is mainly north-south.

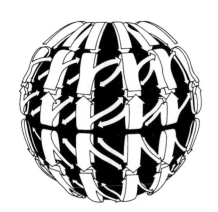

Large-scale airconditioning

The result of this circulation is a flow of heat energy towards the poles and a levelling out of the climate so that both equatorial and polar regions are habitable. The atmosphere generally retains its state of equilibrium as every north-going air current is counter-balanced by a south-going one. In the same way depressions at lower levels

Each hemisphere has three belts of convection cells and the circulation within each belt is greater than it is between them. If the Earth did not rotate, the winds would blow largely in a north-south direction. The Earth's rotation causes them to veer off course (oblique arrows). The model above is schematic and presupposes a planet totally covered by sea. The continents create local wind systems.

in the troposphere are counter-balanced by areas of high pressure in the upper levels, and vice versa. The atmospheric transference of heat is closely associated with the movement of moisture between sea and continent and between different latitudes. Moist air can transport much greater quantities of energy than dry air.

Because the belts of convection cells run east to west, both climate and weather vary according to latitude. Climatic zones are particularly distinguishable at sea where there are no land masses to disturb the pattern.

Man and the winds

For thousands of years mankind has been dependent upon the winds: they brought rain to the land and carried ships across the seas. Thus the westerly wind belts, the trade winds and the monsoon winds of the global circulation systems, have been known to us for many centuries. As recently as the present century Arab ships sailed on the south-west monsoon winds from East Africa to India and back again on the north-east monsoon winds, without need of a compass. The winds alone were sufficient. In the equatorial convergence zone (the "doldrums"), and in the regions around the Tropic of Cancer and Tropic of Capricorn known as the "horse latitudes", sailing ships could drift for weeks unable to steer, while the "roaring forties" of the South Atlantic (40-50°S) were notorious among mariners for their terrible winds.

It was not until the development of the balloon at the end of the 18th century, however, that it became possible to study meteorological conditions at high altitudes. The balloon is still a significant research device although today it carries a radar reflector or a set of instruments and a radio transmitter, rather than the scientists themselves. Nowadays high-flying aircraft and satellites are also important aids to meteorology. Through them we have discovered the west to east jet stream. This blows at speeds of up to 500 km/h at altitudes of 9,000-10,000 m along the border between the Arctic and temperate zone convection belts.

Weather fronts

The circulation within the different convection cells is greater than the exchange of air between them and therefore the temperature in two cells that are close to each other can differ greatly. Consequently the borders between the different convection cells are areas in which warm and cold air masses oppose each other, advancing and withdrawing. In the northern hemisphere the dividing line between the Arctic and temperate convection zones is the polar front, and it is this which determines the weather in northern Europe and North America. This front is unstable, weaving sometimes northward, sometimes southward, of an average latitude of 60°N. Depressions become trapped within the deep concavities of this front and these subsequently move eastward along it with areas of rain and snowfall. In this way global air circulation determines not only the long-term climate but also the immediate weather.

Glossary: **Troposphere:** the part of the atmosphere closest to the surface of the earth
Stratosphere: the atmospheric zone above the troposphere

Questions 1-3

*Complete the diagram using information from the text. Write **NO MORE THAN THREE WORDS** or **ONE NUMBER** in boxes 1-3 on your answer sheet.*

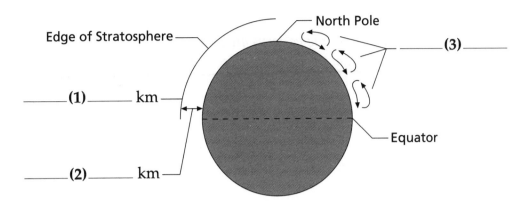

Questions 4-7

Complete the paragraph below using words and phrases from the box. There are more words and phrases than you will need. Write your answers in boxes 4-7 on your answer sheet.

Global air circulation spreads heat from the _____(4)_____ towards the

_____(5)_____. Within this system of heat transfer, climate is affected

not only by _____(6)_____ but also by the amount of moisture in the

air. The most accurate geographical zone in which to study climate is

_____(7)_____ where there are no local wind systems.

on land	equatorial regions
heat	in the air
mountainous regions	latitude
polar regions	at sea
moisture	depressions
coastal regions	longitude

Questions 8-11

Several different wind patterns are mentioned in the passage. For each of the patterns below, write a letter in the boxes marked 8-11 on your answer sheet.

Write:

U	*if the passage states that the patterns are useful*
P	*if the passage states that the patterns present problems*
N	*if the passage does not state whether the patterns are useful or problematic.*

8.   West to east jet stream

9.   The roaring forties

10.   The horse latitudes

11.   North-east monsoon winds

Questions 12-13

*Choose the appropriate letter **A-C** and write it in boxes 12 and 13 on your answer sheet.*

12.   Convection cells near to each other

    A   usually have similar temperatures
    B   usually have slightly different temperatures
    C   may have extremely different temperatures.

13.   The borders between convection cells

    A   are always in the same place
    B   may move forwards and backwards
    C   are totally unpredictable in their position.

Reading Passage 2

You should spend about 20 minutes on Questions 14-26 which are based on Reading Passage 2.

Money as the Unit of Account

Section I

The most difficult aspect of money to understand is its function as a unit of account. In linear measurement we find the definition of a yard, or a metre, easy to accept. In former times these lengths were defined in terms of fine lines etched onto brass rods maintained in standards laboratories at constant temperatures. Money is much more difficult to define, however, because the value of anything is ultimately in the mind of the observer, and such values will change with time and circumstance.

Sir Isaac Newton, as Master of the Royal Mint, defined the pound sterling (£) in 1717 as 113 grains of pure gold. This took Britain off silver and onto gold as defining the unit of account. The pound was 113 grains of pure gold, the shilling was 1/20 of that, and the penny 1/240 of it.

By the end of the nineteenth century the gold standard had spread around most of the trading world, with the result that there was a single world money. It was called by different names in different countries, but all these supposedly different currencies were rigidly interconnected through their particular definition in terms of a quantity of gold.

Section II

In economic life the prices of different commodities and services are always changing with respect to each other. If the potato crop, for example, is ruined by frost or flood, then the price of potatoes will go up. The consequences of that particular price increase will be complex and unpredictable. Because of the high price of potatoes, prices of other things will decline, as demand for them declines. Similarly, the argument that the Middle East crisis following the Iraqi annexation of Kuwait would, because of increased oil prices, have led to sustained general inflation is, although widely accepted, entirely without foundation. With sound money (money whose purchasing power does not decline over time) a sudden price shock in any one commodity will not lead to a general price increase, but to changes in relative prices throughout the economy. As oil increases, other goods and services will drop in price, and oil substitutes will rise in price, as the consequences of the oil price increase work their unpredictable and complex way through the economy.

The use of gold as the unit of account during the days of the gold standard meant that the price of all other commodities and services would swing up and down with reference to the price of gold, which was fixed. If gold supplies diminished, as they did when the 1850s gold rushes in California and Australia petered out, then deflation (a general price level decrease) would set in. When new gold rushes followed in South Africa and again in Australia, in the 1880s and 1890s, the general price level increased, gently, around the world.

Section III

The end of the gold standard began with the introduction of the Bretton-Woods Agreement in 1946. This fixed the value of all world currencies relative to the US dollar, which in turn was fixed to a specific value of gold (US$0.35/oz). However, in 1971 the US government finally refused to exchange US dollars for gold, and other countries soon followed. Governments printed as much paper money or coinage as they wanted, and the more that was printed, the less each unit of currency was worth.

The key problem with these government "fiat" currencies is that their value is not defined; such value is subject to how much money a government cares to print. Their future value is unpredictable, depending as it does on political chance. In our economic calculations concerning the past we automatically convert incomes and expenditures to dollars of a particular year, using CPI deflators which are stored in our computers. When we perform economic calculations into the future we guess at inflation rates and include these guesses in our figures. Our guesses are entirely based on past experience. In Australia most current calculations assume a 3 to 4 per cent inflation rate.

Section IV

The great advantage of the nineteenth-century gold standard was not just that it defined the unit of account, but that it operated throughout almost the entire world. A price in England was the same as a price in Australia and in North America. Anthony Trollope tells us in his diaries about his Australian travels in 1872 that a pound of meat, selling in Australia for twopence, would have cost tenpence or even a shilling in the UK. It was this price difference which drove investment and effort into the development of shipboard refrigeration, and opening up of major new markets for Australian meat, at great benefit to the British public.

Today we can determine price differences between countries by considering the exchange rate of the day. In twelve months' time, even a month's time, however, a totally different situation may prevail, and investments of time and money made on the basis of an opportunity at an exchange rate of the day, become completely wasted because of subsequent exchange rate movements.

The great advantage of having a single stable world money is that such money has very high information content. It tells people where to invest their time, energy and capital, all around the world, with much greater accuracy and predictability than would otherwise be possible.

Glossary: **CPI deflators:** a mathematical calculation based on the Consumer Price Index (CPI) that allows us to compare past prices to current prices.

Questions 14-17

The reading passage has four sections.

Choose the most suitable heading for each section from the list of headings in the box below.
Write the appropriate numbers in boxes 14-17 on your answer sheet.
Note: There are more headings than sections so you will not use all of them.

> i.   the price of gold
> ii.   the notion of money and its expression
> iii. the rise of problematic modern currencies
> iv.   stable money compared to modern "fiat" currencies
> v.   the effects of inflation
> vi.   the interrelationship of prices

14.   SECTION I: _____

15.   SECTION II: _____

16.   SECTION III: _____

17.   SECTION IV: _____

Questions 18-21

Using information from the text, match the following causes with a result. Write the appropriate letters in boxes 18-21 on your answer sheet.

CAUSE	RESULT
18. The price of potatoes goes up.	**A** Oil substitutes become more expensive.
Example *Answer* Oil prices rise. _____ *A* _____	**B** Oil substitutes drop in price.
19. The amount of gold available went up.	**C** People developed techniques of transporting it to other places.
20. The amount of gold available went down.	**D** More people went to live in Australia.
21. Meat in Australia was cheaper than elsewhere.	**E** The price of other things goes down, because fewer people could afford to buy them.
	F People used gold instead of silver as money.
	G All prices went up slightly, everywhere.
	H There is no observable effect.
	I All prices went down, everywhere.

Questions 22-26

In the reading passage, the writer compares money based on a gold standard, and fiat money. Using the information in the passage, match a phrase A, B, or C in List 1 with the writer's opinions in List 2 to show which kind of money is meant.

Write the appropriate letter in boxes 22-26 on your answer sheet.

List 1

A	Money based on a gold standard
B	Government fiat monopoly currencies
C	Both money based on a gold standard and fiat currencies

List 2

22. The writer states that it has a clearly defined value.

23. The writer states that its value by definition varies over time.

24. The writer describes its future value as predictable.

25. The writer knows or can calculate its past value.

26. The writer believes it makes international investment easier.

You should spend about 20 minutes on Questions 27-40 which are based on Reading Passage 3.

Refining Petroleum

Chemically, petroleum is a complex mixture of hydrocarbons (compounds of hydrogen and carbon), with varying amounts of sulphur, nitrogen, oxygen, and traces of some metallic elements appearing in the molecules. Since different groups of hydrocarbons can be used for different purposes (eg. gasoline, kerosene, lubricating oil), the crude petroleum is refined to separate them out. Most petroleum products contain a range of hydrocarbons, and are defined by their boiling range and specific gravity.

Distillation

Distillation was the first method of refining petroleum to be used. Crude oil was placed in horizontal cylindrical stills holding from 100 to 1000 barrels, heat was applied to the bottom of the still, and, at a still-head vapour temperature of about 38°C, light hydrocarbons were distilled and condensed in a pipe coil immersed in a tank of water. As the vapour temperature increased, gasoline was distilled and the condensed vapours were allowed to flow into a receiving tank. When a temperature of about 177°C was reached and a test showed that the specific gravity of the condensate has reached a chosen point, the stream of condensate was directed to a different tank and distillation progressed to a vapour temperature of about 230°C to 260°C to produce a kerosene fraction. When tests showed that the kerosene had all been recovered, the condensate again was diverted to another tank and distillation was continued to produce light fuel-oil distillate, boiling up to about 340°C to 370°C. From this point on, distillation was usually helped by the introduction of steam under the surface so that the partial pressure of the oil vapour was lessened and the temperature of distillation was reduced. This technique was used because the heavier portions of crude oil boiling above light fuel-oil distillates begin to decompose into lighter fractions, or "cracks", at about 405°C with a negative effect on the succeeding distillates and the residual oil in the still.

The early distillation processes were inefficient because no sharp separations of distillate products were obtained. Gasoline contained some kerosene, and kerosene contained both gasoline and higher-boiling distillates belonging in the fuel-oil category. To correct some of this overlapping, redistillation of the primary fractions was practised, sometimes with steam and sometimes with short fractionation columns filled with coarse gravel, lump silica, or other inert material.

Thermal Cracking

The tendency of the heavier portions of crude petroleum to decompose when they are heated above a certain temperature has been put to a most important commercial use in the cracking process. When the higher-boiling fractions of petroleum decompose, carbon-to-carbon bonds are broken and hydrogen is split off from hydrocarbon molecules so that a greater spread of products is obtained than was present in the original crude oil. Cracking makes it possible to increase the yield of gasoline from crude oil by cracking the heavier distillates and residuum left after primary distillation.

Controlled thermal cracking was first applied commercially in 1913. A gas oil distillate was distilled under a pressure of about 520 kilopascals at a temperature of about 400°C. A yield of about 35 per cent of cracked gasoline was obtained. Cracking was continued until the gasoline production waned.

The commercialisation of the cracking process was made necessary by the rapid growth in popularity of the automobile and the ever-growing need for gasoline to fuel it. The problem to refiners was one of increasing the ratio of gasoline to crude oil refined, or else accumulating enormous stocks of other petroleum products that could not be sold.

Catalytic Cracking

As the use of the automobile in the United States expanded, thermal refining processes were unable to yield both the quantity and quality of gasoline needed from a barrel of crude oil. Refiners turned to another technique for increasing yields of gasoline and other light fuels. This process is catalytic cracking.

The first commercially successful catalytic cracking process was developed in the 1930s. In it, granular or pelleted clay particles were used as a catalyst in the cracking chambers. Intermediate-boiling-range petroleum distillates were heated and vapourised and passed through a bed of catalyst to increase the rate of cracking and modify the character of the cracking reactions. Moderate temperatures of from 430° to 480°C were employed, at atmospheric pressure, as opposed to the high pressures of thermal cracking processes.

A further development was the fluid catalytic cracking process, in which finely powdered catalyst was fed into the preheated oil vapours in heavy concentration, so there would be close contact between catalyst and oil vapours in the cracking chambers. The catalyst was carried out of the cracking chamber by the cracked vapours and separated in cyclone separators. It was then purified and returned for further use. The finely powdered catalyst exposed enormously greater surface area than did the pelleted catalyst, hence the improvement in cracking efficiency compared to the original process. The movement of the powdered catalyst inside the reactor and regenerators is accomplished without any interior moving parts and hence no problems of mechanical wear or lubrication of pumps, compressors, valves or other components are encountered.

In the recent past, developments in catalytic cracking have occurred on several fronts. The most significant was the introduction in 1962 of catalysts containing zeolites. The greater activity and selectivity of these "sieve" catalysts make it possible to obtain much higher yields of gasoline fractions - as much as 20 to 30 per cent in some units - than was possible with conventional silica-alumina types.

Glossary: **Catalyst:** a substance that promotes chemical change without itself changing. Many substances, including metals, metal oxides, and various salts, show catalytic properties.
Zeolites: a group of minerals which mostly contain hydrous silicates of lime, soda and alumina.

Questions 27-30

Label the shaded areas on the graph to show what is produced or what event takes place at the different temperatures. Write **NO MORE THAN THREE WORDS** *for each answer. Write your answers in boxes 27-30 on your answer sheet.*

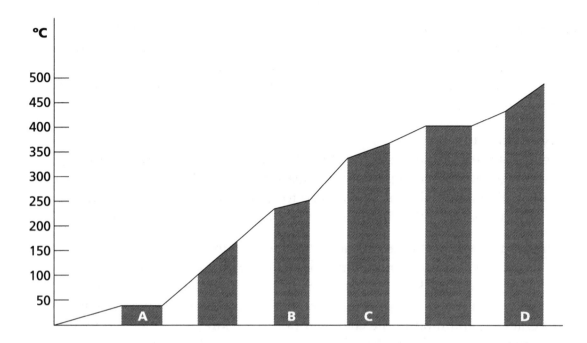

27. Shading A: _____

28. Shading B: _____

29. Shading C: _____

30. Shading D: _____

Questions 31-34

Label the following diagrams using words and phrases from the box below.
Note: there are more words and phrases in the box than you will need. Any word and phrase
may be used more than once. Write the answers in boxes 31-34 on your answer sheet.

thermal cracking	catalyst in powder
distillation	redistillation
catalyst separated out	catalyst in pellets
heavy distillates	catalyst purified
hydrogen separated out	kerosene recovered

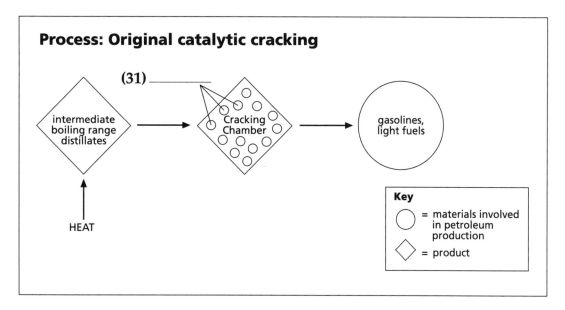

Process: Original catalytic cracking

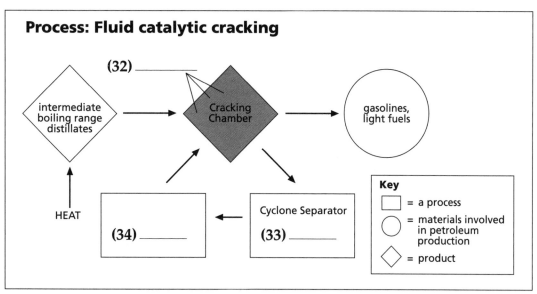

Process: Fluid catalytic cracking

*Complete the following sentences using information from the text. Use **NO MORE THAN THREE WORDS** for each answer. Write your answers in boxes 35-40 on your answer sheet.*

35.   Petroleum products are recognised by their _____ and specific gravity.

36.   In the early days of the petroleum industry, it was often necessary to distill products a second time to _____ them properly.

37 & 38.   Cracking is carried out after _____ using _____ and residuum.

39.   Catalytic cracking is carried out at _____ pressure.

40.   New catalysts have improved the gasoline yield per barrel by _____ %.

Academic Reading Practice Test 2

Reading Passage 1

You should spend about 20 minutes on Questions 1-12 which are based on Reading Passage 1.

Jupiter's Bruises

[In 1994 the comet Shoemaker-Levy 9 collided with the planet Jupiter, causing great excitement in the world of astronomy. The article which follows was written after the first impact.]

Shoemaker-Levy 9 has plunged into Jupiter, and the Hubble Space Telescope has moved away to look at other objects in space. Amateur astronomers, however, are still watching Jupiter to see what bruises were left on the mighty planet by the comet crash of 1994. There was tremendous excitement in astronomical circles during the collision of comet and planet. It is now time to see what has been learned from this impact.

One question which may never be answered: Was Shoemaker-Levy 9 really a comet, or was it an asteroid instead? Comets tend to be a mixture of ice, rock and dust, along with other substances, like carbon monoxide, that evaporate quickly to form a halo and a tail. Scientists studying the chemical composition of the spots on Jupiter where Shoemaker Levy 9 (S-L 9) hit thought they might see evidence of water and oxygen, two of the expected products when an icy comet vaporises. But except for one unconfirmed report, researchers have found only ammonia, hydrogen sulphide and sulphur gas.

Asteroids are rockier than comets. Yet it is possible for an asteroid to have a halo or a tail, made mostly of dust. Says Hal Weaver of the Space Telescope Institute: "The only real evidence that SL-9 was a comet is that it broke apart, and we've never seen that in an asteroid. But maybe this was a fragile asteroid'.

Amateur astronomer David Levy, who with Eugene and Carolyn Shoemaker discovered SL-9, points out that comets were originally distinguished by their appearance. They are objects that look like fuzzy stars with tails, and in any previous century astronomers would have called this discovery a comet. On that basis, argues Levy, "S-L 9 is a comet, period'.

The apparent absence of water at the impact sites provides a clue about how far the SL-9 fragments penetrated Jupiter's atmosphere before exploding. Theorists think that a layer of water vapour lies some 95 km below the visible cloud tops; above the vapour layer, about 50 km down, are clouds believed to consist of a sulphur compound. Since no water seems to have been stirred up, the explosion probably took place in the presumed sulphide layer.

If researchers confirm that the sulphur rose up from Jupiter, it will be "a major discovery," says University of Arizona astronomer Roger Yelle. "We've always believed that much of the colour in Jupiter's clouds comes from sulphur compounds, but we've never detected them."

No one knows why the points of impact are so dark, but it is clear that they are very high up in Jupiter's atmosphere, since the planet's stripes can be seen through them. Astronomers believe the collisions will provide an opportunity to study the winds above Jupiter's cloud tops. The mark left by the first impact is already starting to be spread around. There are also hints of seismic waves - ripples that may have travelled all the way to a dense layer of liquid hydrogen thousands of kilometres down and then bounced back up to the surface, creating rings half the size of the planet's visible face. These waves may offer clues to Jupiter's internal structure.

The spots that were made by the collision will undoubtedly blow away eventually, but it's much too soon to tell if there will be any permanent changes in Jupiter. There is still every chance that the impacts, especially from the four fragments that hit in nearly the same place, will destabilise the atmosphere and create a new, permanent cyclone like Jupiter's Great Red Spot.

It's also possible that the show isn't quite over. Theorists using a computer model argue that debris has lagged behind the original 21 major fragments. These stragglers, they predict, will keep hitting Jupiter for months to come. Unlike the previous fragments the latecomers will smash into the near side of the planet, giving astronomers a chance to watch some strikes directly. Is the theory plausible? Says one astronomer, "We've had so many surprises from S-L 9 already that I wouldn't rule anything out".

Questions 1-7

Do the following statements summarise the opinions of the writer in Reading Passage 1?
In boxes 1-7 of your answer sheet write:

YES	*if the statement agrees with the writer*
NO	*if the statement does not agree with the writer*
NOT GIVEN	*if there is no information about this in the passage*

1. Evidence so far indicates that further study of Shoemaker-Levy will be worthwhile.

2. There are no physical differences between asteroids and comets.

3. The observation of Shoemaker-Levy was an immensely expensive undertaking.

4. David Levy, being an amateur astronomer, was not taken seriously.

5. The dark points of impact indicate there is water on Jupiter.

6. It is now possible to perform detailed studies of Jupiter's internal structure.

7. It is possible that more impacts have occurred since this article was written.

Questions 8-12

Complete the sentences below with words taken from Reading Passage 1. Use **NO MORE THAN THREE WORDS** for each answer. Write your answers in boxes 8-12 of your answer sheet.

8. The comet was observed using the _____ .

9. A comet's tail is usually made up of substances that evaporate quickly such as _____ .

10. Researchers had expected to see evidence of _____ at the impact site, showing the comet's composition.

11. The presence of sulphur compounds may account for the _____ of Jupiter's clouds.

12. The destabilised atmosphere may lead to the formation of another permanent _____ on Jupiter.

Reading Passage 2

You should spend about 20 minutes on Questions 13-26 which are based on Reading Passage 2.

Fashion and Society

In all societies the body is "dressed", and everywhere dress and adornment play symbolic and aesthetic roles. The colour of clothing often has special meaning; a white wedding dress symbolising purity, black clothing indicating remembrance for a dead relative. Uniforms symbolise association with a particular profession. For many centuries purple, the colour representing royalty, was to be worn by no one else. And of course, dress has always been used to emphasise the wearer's beauty, although beauty has taken many different forms in different societies. In the 16th century in Europe, for example, Flemish painters celebrated women with bony shoulders, protruding stomachs and long faces, while women shaved or plucked their hairlines to obtain the fashionable egg-domed forehead. These traits are considered ugly by today's fashion.

The earliest forms of "clothing" seem to have been adornments such as body painting, ornaments, scarifications (scarring), tattooing, masks and often constricting neck and waist bands. Many of these deformed, reformed or otherwise modified the body. The bodies of men and of children, not just those of women, were altered - there seems to be a widespread human desire to transcend the body's limitations, to make it what it is, by nature, not.

Dress in general seems then to fulfil a number of social functions. This is true of modern as of ancient dress. What is added to dress as we ourselves know it in the west is fashion, of which the key feature is rapid and continual changing of styles. The growth of the European city in the 14th century saw the birth of fashionable dress. Previously, loose robes had been worn by both sexes, and styles were simple and unchanging. Dress distinguished rich from poor, rulers from ruled only in that working people wore more wool and no silk, rougher materials and less ornamentation than their masters.

However, by the fourteenth century, with the expansion in trade, the growth of city life, and the increasing sophistication of the royal and aristocratic courts, rapidly changing styles appeared in western Europe. These were associated with developments in tailored and fitted clothing; once clothing became fitted, it was possible to change the styling of garments almost endlessly. By the fifteenth and sixteenth centuries it began to seem shameful to wear outdated clothes, and those who could afford to do so discarded clothing simply because it had gone out of style. Cloth, which was enormously expensive, was literally, and symbolised, wealth in medieval society.

In modern western societies no form of clothing does not feel the impact of fashion; fashion sets the terms of all dress behaviour - even uniforms have been designed by

Paris dressmakers; even nuns have shortened their skirts; even the poor seldom go in rags - they wear cheap versions of the fashions that went out a few years ago and are therefore to be found in second-hand shops and jumble sales.

Even the determinedly unfashionable wear clothes that represent a reaction against what is in fashion. To be unfashionable is not to ignore fashion, it is rather to protest against the social values of the fashionable. The hippies of the 1960s created a unique appearance out of an assortment of secondhand clothes, craft work and army surplus, as a protest against the wastefulness of the consumer society. They rejected the way mass production ignored individuality, and also the wastefulness of luxury.

Looked at in historical perspective the styles of fashion display a crazy relativism. At one time the rich wear cloth of gold embroidered with pearls, at another beige cashmere and grey suiting. In one epoch men parade in elaborately curled hair, high heels and rouge, at another to do so is to court outcast status and physical abuse. It is in some sense inherently ironic that a new fashion starts from rejection of the old and often an eager embracing of what was previously considered ugly. Up to the early twentieth century, the tan had always been the sign of a worker, and therefore avoided by those with pretensions to refinement, who were wealthy enough not to have to work in the sun. However, in the 1920s the tan became the visible sign of those who could afford foreign travel. A tan symbolised health as well as wealth in the 1930s. Recently its carcinogenic dangers have become known, and in any case it is no longer truly chic because many more people than in earlier decades can afford holidays in the sun.

Despite its apparent irrationality, fashion cements social solidarity and imposes group norms. It forces us to recognise that the human body is not only a biological entity, but an organism in culture. To dress the way that others do is to signal that we share many of their morals and values. Conversely, deviations in dress are usually considered shocking and disturbing. In western countries a man wearing a pink suit to a job interview would not be considered for a position at a bank. He would be thought too frivolous for the job. Likewise, even in these "liberated" times, a man in a skirt in many western cultures causes considerable anxiety, hostility or laughter.

However, while fashion in every age is normative, there is still room for clothing to express individual taste. In any period, within the range of stylish clothing, there is some choice of colour, fabric and style. This is even more true last century, because in the twentieth century fashion, without losing its obsession with the new and the different, was mass produced. Originally, fashion was largely for the rich, but since the industrial period the mass-production of fashionably styled clothes has made possible the use of fashion as a means of self-enhancement and self-expression for the majority.

Questions 13-14

*Using information from the text, answer the following questions. Write the appropriate letter **A-D** in boxes 13 and 14 on your answer sheet.*

13. In early times, dress showed the difference between rich and poor in

   A   style of clothing
   B   fabric and decoration of clothing
   C   colour of clothing
   D   cost of clothing.

14. What development in clothing made the concept of fashion possible?

   A   cost of the fabric
   B   shame at outdated clothing
   C   sophistication of decoration
   D   tailored and fitted clothing.

Questions 15-18

*Using information from the text, answer the following questions. **USE NO MORE THAN THREE WORDS** in your answer. Write your answers in boxes 15-18 on your answer sheet.*

15 & 16.   Several unlikely groups of people in the twentieth century are stated to have been affected by fashion. Name TWO of these groups.

17 & 18.   What TWO items of clothing are given as examples of unsuitable clothing for western men to wear?

Questions 19-23

Complete the following table on the early history of fashion, using words and phrases from the box below. Write the appropriate letter **A-J** of your answers in boxes 19-23 on your answer sheet.

A unfashionable clothes thrown away   **F** brightly coloured clothing

B loose robes   **G** simple decorations worn

C fitted clothing   **H** styles began to change slowly

D rapidly changing styles appeared   **I** 15th & 16th centuries

E up to the 14th century   **J** growth of cities

PERIOD	CLOTHING BEHAVIOUR	TYPES OF CLOTHING WORN
Earliest times	_____(19)_____	scars and masks
_____(20)_____	simple, unchanging styles	_____(21)_____
14th century	_____(22)_____	_____(23)_____

The following table contains several of the writer's arguments from the reading passage. Match the argument with the evidence used in the passage to support it by writing the appropriate letter A-I in boxes 24-26 on your answer sheet. One has been done as an example.

Note: there are more statements of evidence than you need.

ARGUMENT	EVIDENCE
Example People who wear unusual or unexpected clothing make other people feel ill at ease. *supported by* ___*B*___	**A** Fashion is now mass-produced.
	B Today people are wary of men who wear bright coloured clothes to work.
24. Clothing can carry symbolic meaning in colour or decoration. *supported by* _____	**C** At some times wealthy people wear bright, heavily ornamented clothes, at some times they wear dark clothing in simple styles.
25. A change in fashion often means accepting what used to be thought unattractive. *supported by* _____	**D** Pale skin became unfashionable and suntanned skin became more fashionable.
	E Many people can afford holidays in the sun.
26. People who wear unfashionable clothes may do so for a reason. *supported by* _____	**F** Black clothes are worn when someone has died.
	G Hippies wore secondhand clothes to protest against wastefulness.
	I Styles were simple and unchanging.

You should spend about 20 minutes on Questions 27-42 which are based on Reading Passage 3.

Mass Production

Car manufacturer Henry Ford's 1908 Model T automobile was his twentieth design over a five-year period that began with the production of the original Model A in 1903. With his Model T, Ford finally achieved two objectives. He had a car that was designed for manufacture, and one that was easily operated and maintained by the owner. These two achievements laid the groundwork for the revolutionary change in direction for the entire motor vehicle industry.

The key to mass production wasn't the moving, or continuous, assembly line. Rather, it was the complete and consistent interchangeability of parts and the simplicity of attaching them to each other. These were the manufacturing innovations that made the assembly line possible. To achieve interchangeability, Ford insisted that the same gauging system be used for every part all the way through the entire manufacturing process. Previously, each part had been made to a slightly different gauge, so skilled fitters had to file each part individually to fit onto the other parts of the car. Ford's insistence on working-to-gauge throughout was driven by his realisation of the payoff he would get in the form of savings on assembly costs. Ford also benefited from recent advances in machine tools able to work on pre-hardened metals. The warping or distortion that occurred as machined parts were being hardened had been the bane of previous attempts to standardise parts. Once the warping problem was solved, Ford was able to develop innovative designs that reduced the number of parts needed and made these parts easy to attach. For example, Ford's four-cylinder engine block consisted of a single, complex casting. Competitors cast each cylinder separately and bolted the four together.

Taken together, interchangeability, simplicity, and ease of attachment gave Ford tremendous advantages over his competition.

Ford's first efforts to assemble his cars, beginning in 1903, involved setting up assembly stands on which a whole car was built, often by one fitter. In 1908, on the eve of the introduction of the Model T, a Ford assembler's average task cycle - the amount of time he worked before repeating the same operations - totalled 514 minutes, or 8.56 hours. Each worker would assemble a large part of a car before moving on to the next. For example, a worker might put all the mechanical parts - wheels, springs, motor, transmission, generator - on the chassis (body), a set of activities that took a whole day to complete. The assembler/fitters performed the same set of activities over and over at their stationary assembly stands. They had to get the necessary parts, file them down so they would fit (Ford hadn't yet achieved perfect interchangeability of parts), then bolt them in place.

The first step Ford took to make this process more efficient was to deliver the parts to each work station. Now the assemblers could remain at the same spot all day. Later in

---

1908, when Ford finally achieved perfect part interchangeability, he decided that the assembler would perform only a single task and move from vehicle to vehicle around the assembly hall. By August of 1913, just before the moving assembly line was introduced, the task cycle for the average Ford assembler had been reduced from 514 to 2.3 minutes. Naturally, this reduction spurred a remarkable increase in productivity, partly because complete familiarity with a single task meant the worker could perform it faster, but also because all filing and adjusting of parts had by now been eliminated. Workers simply popped on parts that fitted every time.

Ford soon recognised the problem with moving the worker from assembly stand to assembly stand: walking, even if only for a yard or two, took time, and jam-ups frequently resulted as faster workers overtook the slower workers in front of them. Ford's stroke of genius in the spring of 1913, at his new Highland Park plant in Detroit, was the introduction of the moving assembly line, which brought the car past the stationary worker. This innovation cut cycle time from 2.3 minutes to 1.19 minutes; the difference lay in the time saved in the worker's standing still rather than walking and in the faster work pace which the moving line could enforce.

Ford's moving assembly consisted of two strips of metal plates - one under the wheels of each side of the car - that ran the length of the factory. At the end of the line, the strips, mounted on a belt, rolled under the floor and returned to the beginning. Since Ford needed only the belt and an electric motor to move it, his cost was minimal - less than $3,500 at Highland Park. The moving assembly speeded up production so dramatically that the savings he could realise from reducing the inventory of parts waiting to be assembled far exceeded this trivial outlay.

Even more striking, Ford's discovery simultaneously reduced the amount of human effort needed to assemble an automobile. What's more, the more vehicles Ford produced, the more the cost per vehicle fell. Even when it was introduced in 1908, Ford's Model T, with its fully interchangeable parts, cost less than its rivals. By the time Ford reached peak production volume of 2 million identical vehicles a year in the early 1920s, he had cut the real cost to the consumer by an additional two-thirds.

To appeal to his target market of average consumers, Ford had also designed unprecedented ease of operation and maintainability into his car. He assumed that his buyer would be a farmer with a modest tool kit and the kinds of mechanical skills needed for fixing farm machinery. So the Model T's owner's manual, which was written in question-and-answer form, explained in sixty-four pages how the owner could use simple tools to solve any of the 140 problems likely to occur with the car.

Ford's competitors were as amazed by this designed-in repairability as by the moving assembly line. This combination of competitive advantages catapulted Ford to the head of the world's motor industry and virtually eliminated craft-production companies unable to match its manufacturing economies. Henry Ford's mass production drove the auto industry for more than half a century and was eventually adopted in almost every industrial activity in North America and Europe.

Using information from the reading passage, fill in the dates on the table below. Write your answers in boxes 27-30 on your answer sheet.

DATE	EVENT
(27) _____	Ford Model A car produced
(28) _____	Ford Model T car began production
(29) _____	Henry Ford introduced the moving assembly line
(30) _____	Ford produced 2 million identical vehicles every year

Questions 31-34

The following boxes summarise improvements in productivity by the Ford company, 1903 to 1913. Show the correct sequence for the improvements by matching A, B, C or D with Stages 1, 2, 3, or 4. Write the appropriate letters A, B, C or D in boxes 31-34 on your answer sheet.

A	• each assembler performed one task only • each assembler moved around the hall from car to car

B	• parts were delivered to each work station • each assembler remained in the same place all day

C	• cars were placed on a moving assembly line • each assembler performed one task only • each assembler remained stationary

D	• each car was built on an assembly stand • each fitter performed many jobs on one car • each fitter collected the necessary parts

31. Stage 1: _____

32. Stage 2: _____

33. Stage 3: _____

34. Stage 4: _____

Questions 35-39

According to the writer in Reading Passage 3, are the following actions an advantage or a disadvantage in mass production?

In boxes 35-39 write:

    A   if the action is stated to be an advantage
    D   if the action is stated to be a disadvantage
    NG if no evaluation is given in the text

35.   Between 1903 and 1908 there were 20 designs of the Ford automobile.

36.   Workers shaped each part to fit individually with all other parts.

37.   Ford's four-cylinder engine block consisted of a single, complex casting.

38.   Workers had complete familiarity with a single task.

39.   Workers collected the necessary parts and took them to their work station.

Questions 40-42

Choose the appropriate letter **A-D** and write it in boxes 40-42 on your answer sheet.

40.   Which graph best describes the change in task time resulting from workers performing a single task only?

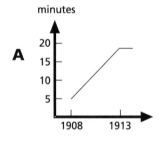
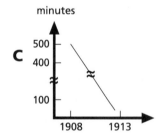
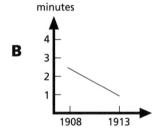
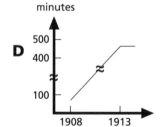

41. Which graph best describes the cost of building a moving assembly line as opposed to the money saved?

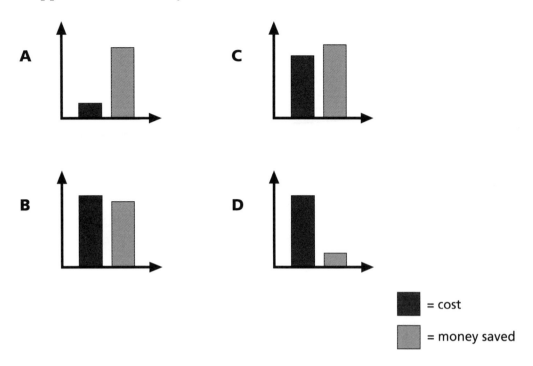

A

C

B

D

■ = cost

▨ = money saved

42. Which graph best describes the relationship between the number of vehicles produced and the cost of the vehicles?

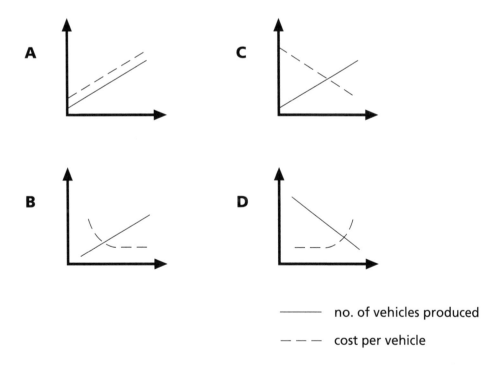

A

C

B

D

——— no. of vehicles produced

– – – cost per vehicle

Academic Reading Practice Test 3

Reading Passage 1

Read the passage below and answer Questions 1-14 that follow.

Myths about Public Speaking

Our fears of public speaking result not only from what we do not know or understand about public communication but also from misconceptions and myths about public encounters. These misconceptions and myths persist among professional people as well as the general public. Let us examine these persistent myths about public communication, which, like our ignorance and misunderstandings of the fundamental assumptions and requirements of public speaking, exacerbate our fears and prevent our development as competent public persons.

A. Perhaps the most dogged and persistent myth about public communication is that it is a "special" activity reserved for unusual occasions. After all, how often do you make a public speech? There are only a few special occasions during the year when even an outgoing professional person will step behind a podium to give a public speech, and many professional people can count on one hand the number of public speeches given in a career. Surely, then, public communication is a rare activity reserved for especially important occasions.

This argument, of course, ignores the true nature of public communication and the nature of the occasions in which it occurs. When we engage with people we do not know well to solve problems, share understanding and perspectives, advocate points of view, or seek stimulation, we are engaged in public speaking. Public communication is a familiar, daily activity that occurs in the streets, in restaurants, in board rooms, courtrooms, parks, offices, factories and meetings.

Is public speaking an unusual activity reserved for special occasions and restricted to the lectern or the platform? Hardly. Rather it is, and should be developed as, an everyday activity occurring in any location where people come together.

B. A related misconception about public communication is the belief that the public speaker is a specially gifted individual with innate abilities and God-given propensities. While most professional people would reject the idea that public speakers are born, not made, they nevertheless often feel that the effective public communicator has developed unusual personal talents to a remarkable degree. At the heart of this misconception - like the myth of public speaking as a "special" activity - is an overly narrow view of what a public person is and does.

Development as an effective public communicator begins with the understanding that you need not be a nationally-known, speak-for-pay, professional platform speaker to be a competent public person. The public speaker is an ordinary person who confronts the necessity of being a public person and uses common abilities to meet the fundamental assumptions and requirements of daily public encounters.

C.   A less widespread but serious misconception of public speaking is reflected in the belief that public speeches are "made for the ages". A public speech is something viewed as an historical event which will be part of a continuing and generally available public record. Some public speeches are faithfully recorded, transcribed, reproduced, and made part of broadly available historical records. Those instances are rare compared to the thousands of unrecorded public speeches made every day.

Public communication is usually situation-specific and ephemeral. Most audiences do well if they remember as much as 40 per cent of what a speaker says immediately after the speaker concludes; even less is retained as time goes by. This fact is both reassuring and challenging to the public communicator. On the one hand, it suggests that there is room for human error in making public pronouncements; on the other hand, it challenges the public speaker to be as informed as possible and to strive to defeat the poor listening habits of most public audiences.

D.   Finally, professional people perhaps more than other groups often subscribe to the misconception that public communication must be an exact science, that if it is done properly it will succeed. The troublesome corollary to this reasoning is that if public communication fails, it is because it was improperly prepared or executed. This argument blithely ignores the vagaries of human interaction. Public speakers achieve their goals through their listeners, and the only truly predictable aspect of human listeners is their unpredictability. Further, public messages may succeed despite inadequate preparation and dreadful delivery.

Professional people often mismanage their fears of public communication. Once we understand what public encounters assume and demand, once we unburden ourselves of the myths that handicap our growth as public persons, we can properly begin to develop as competent public communicators.

Questions 1-5

The reading passage "Myths about Public Speaking" has four sections **A-D**. In boxes 1-5 on your answer sheet write the appropriate letter **A, B, C,** or **D** to show in which section you can find a discussion of the following points. You may use any letter more than once.

1.   A person's ability to be a public speaker.

2.   Whether public speeches are remembered for a long time.

3.   A definition of public speaking.

4.   The relationship of preparation to success in public speaking.

5.   Retention rates as a challenge to public speakers.

Questions 6-11

Do the following statements reflect the claims of the writer in the reading passage?

In boxes 6-11 on your answer sheet write:

YES	if the statement agrees with the writer
NO	if the statement does not agree with the writer
NOT GIVEN	if there is no information about this in the passage

6.   Very few people can become good public speakers.

7.   Public communication is an ordinary daily activity.

8.   Public speaking can be learned at specially designated schools.

9.   Most good public speakers lead happy and productive lives.

10.   It is impossible to predict how a speech will be received.

11.   There is little place for public speaking in the life of the ordinary person.

Questions 12-14

Use information from the reading passage to complete the following sentences. **USE NO MORE THAN THREE WORDS OR A NUMBER**. *Write your answers in boxes 12-14 on your answer sheet.*

12. The writer defines public speaking as any activity where people jointly explore problems, knowledge, attitudes and opinions, or look for _____

13. At the end of most public speeches, most audiences immediately forget about _____ of what they have just heard.

14. Because most public speeches are short-lived, the speaker should work to counteract the _____ of the listeners.

Reading Passage 2

You should spend about 20 minutes on Questions 15-28 which are based on Reading Passage 2.

Environmental Effects of Offshore Drilling and Production

A main public concern about petroleum exploration and production seems to be that a blow-out will cause a major oil spill.

Oil often exists in the subsurface at great pressure and, in the early days, when wells were drilled with only air or water in the hole, the oil could rush into and up the hole and "blow out" at the surface. For reasons of economy and safety, the early oilmen soon put a stop to that practice. Rotary drilling technology developed rapidly, including special drilling fluids with additives to control their density and consistency, and counterbalance the pressure of inflowing oil or gas. Modern drilling rigs are also fitted with blow-out prevention controls - complex systems of metal clamps and shutters which can be used to seal the hole if unexpected high pressures are encountered.

There can be no denying that major blow-outs still occur, and cause loss of life, as well as severe ecological trauma and economic loss. Fortunately, the available technology and proper precautions make them very rare events. Since offshore drilling commenced in Australia in 1965, there has not been a single oil blow-out. Six gas blow-outs occurred during that time - five in Bass Strait and one in the Timor Sea. The Bass Strait blow-outs were all controlled relatively quickly; the Petrel well in the Timor Sea flowed gas for 15 months. Only one well involved any spillage of oil, and the amount was negligible. It is a comment on improving technology and safety procedures that four of the incidents occurred in the 1960s, one in 1971 and the last in 1984.

The statistics on oil spills from offshore exploration and production in Australian Commonwealth waters are shown in the table below. The total spillage, over 26 years, is roughly equivalent in size to a large backyard swimming pool. The main spills have actually occurred in the loading of fuel onto production platforms; they had nothing to do with the oilwell itself.

AUSTRALIAN DRILLING RECORD		
Total number of incidents on offshore facilities from 1965 to 1991, involving spills >320 litres, or causing injury or damage 51	Total number of wells drilled	1,100
	Total number of kilolitres (barrels) of oil produced	480,000,000 (3,100,000,000)
• Platform oil spills 27 • Explosions and fires 13 • Blow-out 6 • Pipeline breaks and leaks 2 • Other 3	Total number of kilolitres (barrels) spilt	70 (440)
	Largest single spill in kilolitres (barrels)	10 (63)

Source: *Oil Spills in the Commonwealth of Australia offshore areas connected with Petroleum Exploration and Development Activities.*
Department of Primary Industries and Energy

In addition to the oil spill issue, there are concerns about other discharges from the drilling and production facilities: sanitary and kitchen wastes, drilling fluid, cuttings and produced water.

Putrescible sanitary and kitchen wastes are discharged into the ocean but must be processed in accordance with regulations set by the Federal government. This material is diluted rapidly and contributes to the local food chain, without any risk of nutrient oversupply. All solid waste material must be brought ashore.

The cuttings are sieved out of the drilling fluid and usually discharged into the ocean. In shallower waters they form a low mound near the rig; in deeper water a wider-spread layer forms, generally within one kilometre of the drillsite, although this depends on a number of factors. Some benthic (bottom-dwelling) organisms may be smothered, but this effect is local and variable, generally limited to within about 100 metres of the discharge point. Better-adapted organisms soon replace them and storm-driven wave activity frequently sweeps away the material.

Drilling fluid is also discharged directly into the ocean. Most of the common constituents of water-based fluids used in Australia have low-to-nil toxicity to marine organisms. Some additives are toxic but are used in small concentrations and infrequently. The small amounts of heavy metals present are not absorbed into the bodies of marine organisms, and therefore it is unlikely that they would pose a problem for animals higher up the food chain. Field studies have shown that dilution is normally very rapid, ranging to 1,000-fold within 3 metres of the discharge point. At Rivoli-1 well in Exmouth Gulf, the input was chemically undetectable 560 metres away.

Oil-based drilling fluids have a more toxic component, and discharge to the marine environment is more significant. However, they are used only rarely in Australia, and the impact remains relatively local. At Woodside's North Rankin A Platform offshore Western Australia, the only facility currently using oil-based fluids, the discharge is diluted 2,000-fold within 1 kilometre downcurrent, and undetectable beyond 200 metres either side.

In the event of a discovery, the presence of a permanent production facility and the discharge of "produced water" are additional concerns. Produced water is the water associated with the oil or gas deposit, and typically contains some petroleum, dissolved organic matter and trace elements. Most produced water is effectively non-toxic but, even when relatively toxic, is quickly diluted to background levels. The impact occurs mainly within about 20 metres of the discharge point, but is observable in some instances for about 1 kilometre downcurrent. Government regulations limit the oil content allowed to be discharged, and the produced water is treated on the platforms to meet those specifications. The discharge points are carefully selected to maximise dispersion and dilution, and avoid any particularly sensitive local environments.

Ultimately the best test of the real environmental effect of drilling and producing operations may be the response of the environment to the fixed production platforms. In many areas the platforms quickly become artificial reefs, with the underwater supports of the platforms providing a range of habitats, from sea-bottom to surface, and quickly colonised by a wide range of marine plants and animals.

Glossary: **Cuttings:** small pieces of rock broken off as the drill cuts through the rock
Putrescible: able to decompose, rot, break down

Questions 15-17

Choose the appropriate letter A-D and write it in boxes 15-17 on your answer sheet.

15.   Oil sometimes "blows out" of a drilling hole because

    A   the oil is mixed up with air
    B   special drilling fluids are used
    C   the surface pressure is greater than the pressure under the ground
    D   oil exists under pressure under the ground.

16.   Sudden high pressures

    A   cannot be controlled
    B   can be controlled using metal clamps and shutters
    C   can be controlled using water to counterbalance the pressure of the oil
    D   can be controlled using rubber pressure valves.

17.   Since offshore drilling began in Australia in 1965

    A   oil and gas blow-outs have been a major problem
    B   oil blow-outs have occurred occasionally
    C   most gas blow-outs were rapidly controlled
    D   gas blow-outs have occurred regularly up to the present.

Questions 18-20

Answer the questions below **USING NO MORE THAN THREE WORDS OR A NUMBER**. Write your answers in boxes 18-20 on your answer sheet.

18. How much oil was spilt in the largest accident on offshore facilities?

19. How many incidents were the result of blow-outs?

20. According to the table, what was the major cause of spillage of oil?

Questions 21-28

Using the information in the passage, identify each type of waste described below. In boxes 21 to 28 on your answer sheet, write

SK-1	if the statement refers to	sanitary and kitchen wastes which decay
SK-2	if the statement refers to	solid sanitary and kitchen wastes
C	if the statement refers to	cuttings
DW	if the statement refers to	drilling fluid - water-based
DO	if the statement refers to	drilling fluid - oil-based
PW	if the statement refers to	produced water

Note: each indicator may be used more than once. An example has been done for you.

> *Example*   This waste is one thousand times weaker at a point three metres from where it enters the ocean.
>
> *Answer*   **DW**

21. This waste must not be discharged into the ocean.

22. This waste may contain heavy metals and toxic additives.

23. This waste can be used as a food source by marine organisms.

24. This waste is produced at only one location in Australian waters.

25. This waste consists of solids which are usually deposited on the ocean floor near the drilling rig.

26. This waste may sometimes cause problems due to its petroleum content.

27. This waste consists of substances very slightly poisonous or not poisonous at all to sea life, although substances added to it may be more harmful.

28. Because this waste contains oil, its discharge is carefully controlled to protect vulnerable marine ecosystems.

Reading Passage 3

You should spend about 20 minutes on Questions 29-42 which are based on Reading Passage 3.

Garbage In, Garbage Out

There are many ways of obtaining an understanding of people's behaviour. One of these is to study the objects discarded by a community, objects used in daily lives. The study of the refuse of a society is the basis for the science of archaeology in which the lives and behaviour of past societies are minutely examined. Some recent studies have indicated the degree to which rubbish is socially defined.

For several years the University of Arizona, USA, has been running a Garbage Project, in which garbage is collected, sorted out and noted. It began in 1973 with an arrangement whereby the City of Tucson collected for analysis garbage from randomly selected households in designated census collection districts. Since then the researchers have studied other cities, both in the USA and Mexico, refining their techniques and procedures in response to the challenges of validating and understanding the often unexpected results they have obtained. Garbage is sorted according to an extremely detailed schedule, a range of data for each item is recorded on a standardised coding form, and the researchers cross-tabulate their findings with information from census and other social surveys.

This Project arose out of courses designed to teach students at the University the principles of archaeological methodology and to sensitise them to the complex and frequently surprising links between cultural assumptions and physical realities. Often a considerable discrepancy exists between what people say they do - or even think they do - and what they actually do. In one Garbage Project study, none of the Hispanic (Spanish-speaking) women in the sample admitted to using as much as a single serving of commercially-prepared baby food, clearly reflecting cultural expectations about proper mothering. Yet garbage from the Hispanic households with infants contained just as many baby food containers as garbage from non-Hispanic households with infants.

The Project leaders then decided to look not only at what was thrown away, but what happened to it after that. In many countries waste is disposed of in landfills; the rubbish is compacted and buried in the ground. So in 1987, the Project expanded its activities to include the excavation of landfills across the United States and Canada. Surprisingly, no-one had ever attempted such excavations before.

The researchers discovered that far from being sites of chemical and biological activity, the interiors of waste landfills are rather inactive, with the possible exception of those established in swamps. Newspapers buried 20 or more years previously usually remained perfectly legible, and a remarkable amount of food wastes of similar age also remained intact.

While discarded household products such as paints, pesticides, cleaners and cosmetics result in a fair amount of hazardous substances being contained in municipal landfills, toxic leachates pose considerably less danger than people fear, provided that a landfill is properly sited and constructed. Garbage Project researchers have found that the leachates do not migrate far, and tend to get absorbed by the other materials in the immediate surrounds.

The composition of landfills is also strikingly different from what is commonly believed. In a 1990 US survey people were asked whether particular items were a major cause of garbage problems. Disposable nappies (baby diapers) were identified as a major cause by 41 per cent of the survey respondents, plastic bottles by 29 per cent, all forms of paper by six per cent, and construction debris by zero per cent. Yet Garbage Project data shows that disposable nappies make up less than two per cent of the volume of landfills and plastic bottles less than one per cent. On the other hand, over 40 per cent of the volume of landfills is composed of paper and around 12 per cent is construction debris.

Packaging - the paper and plastic wrapping around goods bought - has also been seen as a serious cause of pollution. But while some packaging is excessive, the Garbage Project researchers note that most manufacturers use as little as possible, because less is cheaper. They also point out that modern product packaging frequently functions to reduce the overall size of the solid-waste stream.

This apparent paradox is illustrated by the results of a comparison of garbage from a large and socially diverse sample of households in Mexico City with a similarly large and diverse sample in three United States cities. Even after correcting for differences in family size, US households generated far less garbage than the Mexican ones. Because they are much more dependent on processed and packaged foods than Mexican households, US households produce much less food debris. (And most of the leaves, husks, etc. that the US processor has removed from the food can be used in the manufacture of other products, rather than entering the waste stream as is the likely fate with fresh produce purchased by households.)

One criticism made of Western societies is that the people are wasteful, and throw things away while they are still useable. This, however, does not seem to be true. Garbage Project data showed that furniture and consumer appliances were entering the solid waste stream at a rate very much less than would be expected from production and service-life figures. So the researchers set up a study to track the fate of such items and thus gained an insight into the huge informal and commercial trade in used goods that rarely turns up in official calculations and statistics.

The Garbage Project's work shows how many misconceptions exist about garbage. The researchers are therefore critical of attempts to promote one type of waste management, such as source reduction or recycling, over others, such as incineration or landfilling. Each has its advantages and disadvantages, and what may be appropriate for one locality may not be appropriate for another.

Glossary: **Leachate:** water carrying impurities which has filtered through the soil

---

Questions 29-35

Complete the following notes using information from the passage. Write NO MORE THAN THREE WORDS OR A NUMBER in boxes 29-35 on your answer sheet.

The Garbage Project

- started in 1973

- organised by ____(Example)____   Answer: *University of Arizona*

- first studied garbage in the city of _____(29)_____ since then has studied it in other cities in USA and _____(30)_____

- method: garbage collected and sorted, the information noted on _____(31)_____

- findings compared with _____(32)_____ and other social surveys

- reason for Project: show students the _____(33)_____ of archaeological _____(34)_____

- from 1987 Garbage Project studied _____(35)_____ in USA and Canada

---

Questions 36-39

Complete the following sentences using information in the passage. Choose the appropriate phrase A-C from the list in the box and write its letter in boxes 36-39 on your answer sheet. You may use any phrase more than once.

A	more ... than
B	less ... than, fewer ... than
C	as many ... as, as much ... as

36. Hispanic women used _____ baby food _____ they said they did.

37. After excavating landfills the Garbage Project researcher found that there were _____ plastic bottles _____ people thought.

38. Mexican families create _____ garbage _____ American families.

39. Consumer appliances are reused _____ _____ was officially predicted.

Questions 40-42

Below are some of the wrong ideas that the passage states people have about garbage. Match each misconception I-IV with TWO counterarguments A-M used in the passage to argue against them. Write the appropriate letters A-M in boxes 40-42 on your answer sheet.

MISCONCEPTIONS	COUNTERARGUMENTS
Example I. Landfills are dangerous because they are full of germs and chemicals.	**A** 40% of landfills is paper
	B perishable items are often almost unchanged, even after long periods of time
II. Household items, like disposable nappies, are a major cause of garbage problems.	**C** people throw away furniture and consumer appliances
	D processing and packaging cuts down on other garbage
III. Packaging is wasteful, and causes excess garbage.	**E** chemicals become less dangerous after 20 years
	F disposable nappies make up less than 2% of landfills
IV. Western societies waste many useable items.	**G** fresh food creates less waste debris
	H chemicals do not spread far in landfills
	I plastic bottles are a bigger waste problem than nappies
	J there are many businesses that collect and resell things people no longer want
	K manufacturers cut their costs by using as little packaging as possible
	L household goods constituted a smaller than expected part of solid waste
	M people use fewer disposable nappies now than in past years

Example
Counter arguments for Misconception I: *B & H*

Counter arguments for Misconception II: _____(40)_____

Counter arguments for Misconception III: _____(41)_____

Counter arguments for Misconception IV: _____(42)_____

Academic Reading Practice Test 4

Reading Passage 1

You should spend about 20 minutes on Questions 1-16 which are based on Reading Passage 1.

Hazardous Compound Helps to Preserve Crumbling Books

Librarians may be able to save millions of books from slowly crumbling with a new chemical process that uses a hazardous flammable compound, diethyl zinc (DEZ). Chemists in the US have successfully completed an 18-month trial of the technique, which neutralises the acids in paper which cause books to decay.

The method was developed by the Dutch chemical giant, Akzo, in collaboration with the US Library of Congress. It can treat 1,000 books at a time at a fraction of the cost of microfilming.

The world's libraries and archives are today stocked mainly with books that are destroying themselves because of a new way of making paper that was introduced in the middle of the last century. In this process, wood pulp became the main source of the cellulose from which paper was made, replacing the cotton or linen rags used previously.

Unfortunately, book publishers were unaware that wood pulp's slight acidity would eventually threaten their work. The acid attacks the cellulose polymer of paper, breaking it down into shorter and shorter pieces until the paper's structure collapses.

The only answer is to neutralise the acids in the paper by chemical means. This has generally been done by unbinding the book, treating it page by page with a carbonate solution, and then rebinding it. The cost can be as much as £200 per volume. Akzo's method can be done without taking the binding off the book.

On the face of it, DEZ would seem the last chemical that should be brought in contact with paper. This volatile liquid bursts into flames when it comes in contact with air. However, it is not DEZ's sensitivity to oxidation which is the key to its use as a preserving agent, but its ability to neutralise acids by forming zinc salts with them.

Because DEZ is volatile it permeates the pores in paper. When it meets an acid molecule, such as sulphuric acid, it reacts to form zinc sulphate and ethane gas. DEZ is such a strong base that it will react with any acid, including the weaker organic ones. It will also react with any residual water in the paper to form zinc oxide. This is an added bonus for the book conservators, since it buffers the paper against future permeation by acidic gases from the atmosphere such as sulphur dioxide.

Not only will DEZ protect against acid attack but it is also capable of neutralising alkalis, which threaten some kinds of paper. It can do this because zinc oxide is amphoteric - capable of reacting with either acids or alkalis.

The Akzo method treats closed books and protects every page. It adds about 2 per cent of zinc oxide to the weight of the book. Much of this is deposited near the edges of the pages, the parts which are most affected by the acid from readers' fingers or environmental pollution. The only risk in the Akzo process comes from the DEZ itself; this caused a fire at NASA's Goddard Space Flight Center where earlier tests on the method were carried out.

For the process, the books are gently heated under vacuum for a day to remove residual traces of moisture. The chamber is then flushed with dry nitrogen gas for five hours to remove the remaining air before DEZ is introduced at a low pressure into the gas stream. DEZ is passed through for about eight hours. Unreacted DEZ is trapped out of the exit gases and recycled, while the ethane is burned off.

When the process is complete, the chamber is purged with nitrogen to remove residual DEZ. The whole process takes about three days. The cost per book is about £2, considerably less even than the £40 for microfilming.

This work was originally funded by the US Library of Congress, which has over 10 million books now at risk. According to Dick Miller, Akzo's director for book preservation, tests have shown that the method can deal with hundreds of books at a time. A million books a year could be rescued by the new process, for which Akzo has been granted exclusive rights. The treated books should then survive for hundreds of years.

Another national institution, the British Library, launched an adopt-a-book scheme to help it meet the costs of processing books. The British Library has so far raised over £80,000. But if the traditional method is used, this will barely cover a twentieth of 1 per cent of the 2 million books the Library needs to treat.

Edmund King of the British Library's preservation service says that the Library has developed another method which coats the individual fibres of the paper with ethyl acrylate polymer, protecting the books not only against acid attack but actually making them stronger. The British Library is now seeking an industrial partner to exploit its work.

Questions 1-4

Do the following statements summarise the opinions of the writer in Reading Passage 1? In boxes 1-4 of your answer sheet write:

YES	*if the statement agrees with the writer*
NO	*if the statement does not agree with the writer*
NOT GIVEN	*if there is no information about this in the passage*

1. The Akzo preservation method is more expensive than the traditional method.

2. The Akzo preservation method can treat more books at one time than the traditional method.

3. The US Library of Congress must treat more books than the British Library.

4. The traditional preservation method adds more weight to the book than the Akzo method.

Questions 5-8

The text describes a chemical, diethyl zinc (DEZ). From the list below, choose 4 attributes of DEZ as described in the passage. Write the appropriate letters A-H in any order in boxes 5-8 on your answer sheet.

Attributes of DEZ

- **A** It bursts into flames when it comes in contact with air.
- **B** It forms a protective layer of zinc oxide on the surface of the paper.
- **C** It changes acid into zinc sulphate throughout the paper.
- **D** It reacts with acids to produce zinc salts and water.
- **E** It can react with both acids and alkalis.
- **F** The chemical reactions it causes make books heavier.
- **G** It coats the fibres of the paper with ethyl acrylate polymer.
- **H** It tends to retain water within the paper structure.

The four attributes of DEZ are:

5. _____

6. _____

7. _____

8. _____

Questions 9-16

Complete the following flowcharts using phrases from the box below. Write the appropriate letter A-L in boxes 9-16 on your answer sheet. There are more phrases than you will need. Each phrase may be used more than once.

A	Books are cooled
B	Books are heated
C	Unused / leftover DEZ gas removed
D	Unused / leftover DEZ gas burned
E	Unused / leftover DEZ gas reused
F	Dry nitrogen gas is circulated
G	Each page treated with carbonate solution
H	Each page treated with DEZ
I	Akzo preservation method
J	British Library preservation method
K	Ethane gas removed and burned
L	Traditional preservation method

Book Preserving Process: _____(9)_____

Take book apart ⟶ _____(10)_____ ⟶ book put together again

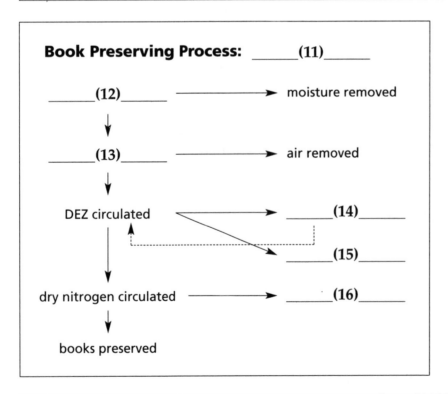

Book Preserving Process: _____(11)_____

_____(12)_____ ⟶ moisture removed

_____(13)_____ ⟶ air removed

DEZ circulated ⟶ _____(14)_____

_____(15)_____

dry nitrogen circulated ⟶ _____(16)_____

books preserved

Reading Passage 2

You should spend about 20 minutes on Questions 17-31 which are based on Reading Passage 2.

Drugs and Obesity

Thin is in, in America. Not only fashion magazines, but also doctors proclaim the importance of a slim, healthy body. Yet despite the current obsession with the trim, taut and terrific body, Americans are putting on weight. In studies conducted in 1980, one quarter of Americans were found to be overweight. Fifteen years later, that number had risen to one third of the population.

In the past, doctors have always recommended a combination of diet and exercise to combat obesity. With the increase in the number of people who are overweight, however, this solution is increasingly being seen to be ineffective.

Given that diet and exercise often do not help produce weight loss, scientists are becoming convinced that, for many, obesity is a genetic disorder. In 1994 a research group at Rockefeller University discovered in experiments on mice what is now called the obesity, or "ob" gene. In turn this discovery led to the identification of a hormone, termed leptin, that signals to the brain the amount of fat stored in the body. When injected into the rodents, the hormone reduced appetite and increased the body's utilisation of calories, the energy produced by food which the body may convert to fat. With findings like these, a large number of medical experts are turning to a selection of drugs which appear to be safe and effective in reducing weight and maintaining lower weight levels.

Because they see obesity as an illness, these authorities claim that treatment should involve not only diet and exercise but drugs as well. What they have in mind is not just a short course of medication to produce small degrees of weight loss. They want to prescribe long-term, perhaps lifetime, drug therapies, just as they might for high blood pressure or diabetes. Obesity's victims, these doctors hope, will not only be able to lose weight, but will also keep that weight off forever.

Not everyone in the medical community is satisfied with the new therapies. Conservatives are seriously worried that the new drugs are, in fact, merely placebos ("medicines" that have no medical effect but may benefit the patient psychologically), or, worse, are actually detrimental to patients' health. Their concerns are understandable. A few decades ago amphetamines - nicknamed "uppers" or "speed" - were widely prescribed to control weight. Patients became slimmer, but suffered from tension and irritability, higher pulse rates, and sleepless nights, side effects that may have outweighed the medical benefits of lower body weight. Conservatives also point out that risky as amphetamines were, they were generally prescribed only for temporary use. Advocates of new drug treatments leave open the possibility that the medications will be prescribed for a lifetime.

While there are at least 5 new diet drugs waiting approval by the US Drug and Food Administration, at the moment, the only diet medication that is normally used in the US is "fen-phen", a combination of the drugs fenfluramine and phentermine. Fenfluramine boosts serotonin, which elevates mood, while phentermine mimics other substances in the brain. Together, the drugs suppress appetite and increase the rate of burning of calories. As its success becomes more widely known, demand for this medication is increasing. Prescriptions for fenfluramine in 1995 were expected to be four times what they were the previous year.

For several reasons, however, fen-phen is not the perfect diet medication. First, there is some debate over safety, although most fen-phen researchers say the drugs pose minor health risks compared with amphetamines. For most patients the short-term side effects are negligible; phentermine heightens alertness while persuading the body to burn more calories, and fenfluramine, thought to cut cravings for starches and sweets, can cause drowsiness. But some users experience a racing heartbeat and, although rarely, high blood pressure. While its effects are milder than those of amphetamines, the feeling of higher energy that fen-phen stirs can be habit-forming. Used alone, phentermine has enough kick to appeal to recreational drug users, who call it "bumblebee". Perhaps even more importantly for dieters, while the drug may cause initial weight loss, over a period of several years, subjects taking the drugs tended to regain some of the weight they had lost - although at a slower rate than those who did not take fen-phen.

Many conservative doctors, moreover, still remain reluctant to diagnose obesity as a disease. In a 1987 survey of 318 physicians, two thirds said their obese patients lacked self-control, and 39% described them as lazy. This traditional view holds that obesity results from a lack of discipline, correctable by diet and exercise. Since studies show that most dieters eat more than they say - or even think - they do, there is probably some truth in seeing a much simpler cause.

On the other hand, the traditional view is challenged by the discovery of the ob gene, which would seem to place significant weight loss outside the individual's control. Then there is the problem of the ever-increasing numbers of obese people, with the resulting increase in hypertension, and diabetes, leading to kidney failure and heart disease. All of these conditions require medication, if not costly equipment and surgery. If all of these effects of obesity must be treated with medication, why refuse medical treatment to help control body weight? Is not prevention better than a cure?

Questions 17-20

Choose the appropriate letter A-D and write it in boxes 17-20 on your answer sheet.

17. A hormone called leptin has recently been discovered. According to the passage, this hormone

   A   increases drowsiness
   B   increases appetite
   C   increases fat production
   D   improves the use of energy from food.

18. Conservative doctors do not like the drug therapies for obesity because

   A   they are based on amphetamines
   B   they are expensive
   C   they may be taken for long periods of time
   D   they cause kidney failure.

19. The number of drug-based diet treatments used at present in the US is

   A   5, including amphetamines
   B   5, not including amphetamines
   C   1
   D   none.

20. One disadvantage of fen-phen is that

   A   taken long term, people tended to gain weight previously lost
   B   it can only be taken for short periods of time
   C   it causes irritability and sleeplessness
   D   too many people use it.

Questions 21-23

*Below are some of the treatments commonly used to treat obesity. Match each treatment with ONE disadvantage mentioned in the text by writing the letter **A-G** in boxes 21-23 on your answer sheet.*

TREATMENTS
21. Traditional weight loss methods
22. Amphetamines
23. Fen-phen

DISADVANTAGES	
A	excessive weight loss
B	kidney failure
C	low blood pressure
D	possibly addictive
E	rapid beating of the heart
F	dizziness
G	regularly ineffective

Questions 24-31

*Complete the paragraph below using words and phrases, marked **A-L**, from the box below. There are more words and phrases than you will need. You may use any word or phrase more than once. Write the appropriate letters **A-L** in boxes 24-31 on your answer sheet.*

Some doctors in the USA believe that obesity should be treated, like any illness, with ____(24)____ , but many conservative doctors see obesity as mainly controllable through ____(25)____. These doctors are concerned by the use of ____(26)____ to treat obesity for several reasons. Firstly, many cause ____(27)____ which can diminish the benefits of weight loss. Furthermore, these doctors believe that such treatments should be used for ____(28)____ but many drug therapists are prepared to use them for ____(29)____

On the other hand, there is evidence that obesity is related to the body's production of ____(30)____ and therefore is an illness. Recent discoveries of ____(31)____ in fact go further and seem to remove responsibility for obesity from individuals.

A weight loss	G body fat
B short periods of time	H drug therapies
C diet and exercise	I hormones
D an illness	J weight gain
E calories	K the "ob" gene
F side effects	L long periods of time

Reading Passage 3

You should spend about 20 minutes on Questions 32-42 which are based on Reading Passage 3.

The Introduction of the Aged Pension in Australia

Australia was settled by Europeans in 1788, mainly to house criminals, but with a few independent farmers and business men. The settlements were not wealthy, and there was little help available to those in need: the poor, the sick, the unemployed, the aged. To begin with, what little help was available came in the form of charity: donations of money, accommodation or medical treatment to selected needy. A second approach that began to emerge in the late nineteenth century was that of "universalism". It stressed that all people in society should be entitled to certain benefits - up to a minimum level and across a restricted range of services. This approach was eventually used to argue for the introduction of a pension for the aged poor.

It was an area of welfare which had been the subject of active debate in England since the mid-1880s or earlier. A number of proposals were discussed in England, and by the mid-1890s, in Sydney. These included schemes based on voluntary contributions of money to an insurance fund during working years, on various proportionate compulsory contributions from employer and employee, or on the payment from the state to a defined category of people. The German scheme of compulsory health and unemployment insurance payments from worker, employer and the state, was also examined.

It should be noticed that the proportion of the colonies' populations over 65 years of age was rising steadily. In 1861 in New South Wales it had been 1.4 per cent; by 1891 this had risen to 2.5 per cent, and by 1901 was 3.4 per cent. In absolute numbers in 1901, that was over 46,500 people. In general terms, there was a 60 per cent increase in the ten years from 1891 to 1901 in the number of people over the age of 65 living in the colonies, a rate of growth about twice as fast as that of the general population of the colonies. This demographic fact set the scene for consideration of the problem of the aged poor.

In New South Wales the difficulties of the depression of the 1890s encouraged the Benevolent Society, the largest charity in the state, to support the idea of an age pension because this would ease its own burden. However, it took the positive action of humanitarians to get the movement going. J.C. Neild was both a free-trade politician and an insurance company officer with some experience of the actual conditions of poverty of working-class people struggling to maintain respectability as the implications of age loomed large in their lives. He knew at first hand how difficult it was for such people to maintain insurance policies, however modest. He pressed for action in 1895 to "empty the barracks" (large dormitories to house the poor) of their aged inmates, barracks already so full and overcrowding rapidly. Canon Bertie Boyce and Sir Arthur Renwick added Christian support and energy, convening an important public meeting and promoting the idea in the press. Then the Labor (socialist) Party took up the idea early in 1896. Government administrators involved in poor relief, such as Sydney Maxted, supported the idea too, because they believed it would be cheaper than institutional care. In 1896 the government therefore selected a group of politicians, a Select Committee, to examine the question of state insurance, old age pensions and invalidity. The Committee found government and voluntary organisers welcoming a pension for the aged as another means of helping the poor, as well as emptying the barracks and saving money. But the chairman of the committee, E.W. O'Sullivan, put an entirely different interpretation on the matter. He did not regard an aged pension as an addition to the instruments of selective charity. He argued in the report for a pension funded by specific community taxes, not one tied to employment or to voluntary contributions. He wanted a pension which, moreover, would be:

> A free gift from the State ...[to those] who have for a fair period assisted to create our civilisation, aided in the development of the resources of the country, and helped to bear the public burdens of the community by the payment of taxes.

Here was a firm assertion of the universal principle of entitlement based on citizenship. The Select Committee's report also contained enough limitations about potential recipients to make it politically acceptable. It was, with all its ambiguities and qualifications, the working basis of a universalist approach to the problem of caring for the aged poor which asserted a clear claim on their behalf to some degree of dignity and independence as a right. Instead of chancy selective charity leading to early institutionalisation and consequent physical decay, here was an opportunity for social action on a consistent, statutory basis, taking existing family life as its foundation.

The New South Wales Old Age Pensions Act came into being in 1900, followed over the next few years by similar acts in the other states. It was not till 1908 that these quite disparate state arrangements were replaced by Commonwealth (federal) legislation. There were, as almost always in universalist schemes, financial criteria. Only a specific category of citizens would benefit. Income in excess of £52 per annum or property valued in excess of £310 would deny the pension, while income between £26 and £52 per annum proportionately reduced the pension.

It is clear that the Commonwealth government of the time, led by Deakin for the Labor Party, shared a radical view of social forces which emphasised the problems outside individual control, and the paternal responsibility of the government to acknowledge the universal rights of its citizens. The older tradition of liberal individualism which set such store by self-improvement and personal responsibility was not widely upheld in the federal area. Nor should it be forgotten that the worst of the drought of the 1890s was past, and federal government income was buoyant. Arising out of that complex of idealism and pragmatic search for workable cash benefits, the Commonwealth old age pension came into being on 1 July 1909, bringing years of bureaucratic and political manoeuvre to cope with its application, extension or even containment, during which some of the difficulties of universalism were to be vividly revealed.

Questions 32-37

Complete the sentences using numbers from the text. Write your answers in boxes 32-37 on your answer sheet.

32.   In 1901, the proportion of people over 65 was _____

33 & 34.   From _____ to _____ the number of aged people increased much faster than the general population in Australia.

35.   When the pension was first introduced, people with property worth more than _____ would not be able to get a pension.

36 & 37.   When the pension was first introduced, people earning more than _____ and less than _____ would only receive a portion of the pension.

Questions 38-41

*In the reading passage, several opinions on care for the aged are discussed. These opinions are summarised in the sentences below. Answer questions 38-41 by writing the **NAME** of the person or philosophy supporting each idea in boxes 38-41 on your answer sheet.*

38.   Every person in society has the right to receive certain benefits.

39.   It is less expensive to pay pensions than to care for the elderly poor in government facilities.

40.   Older people deserve a pension because of the contribution they have made to society throughout their lives.

41.   It is up to people to look after themselves and to improve their own lives.

Question 42

In box 42 on your answer sheet, write the name of the philosophy of social responsibility that ultimately provided the basis for the Australian old age pension scheme.

42.   _____

Academic Reading Practice Test 5

Reading Passage 1

Questions 1-12

You should spend about 20 minutes on Questions 1-12 which are based on Reading Passage 1.

Questions 1-4

The reading passage below has five sections.

Choose the most suitable heading for each section from the list of headings below. Write the appropriate numbers (i-viii) in boxes 29-32 on your answer sheet.

NB There are more headings than sections, so you will not use all of them. You may use any of the headings more than once.

List of headings

(i)	The workers and their families
(ii)	The managers of the Snowy Mountains Scheme
(iii)	The workers' problems
(iv)	The unique nature of the scheme
(v)	Why the Snowy Mountains Scheme began
(vi)	The people who came to the Snowy Mountains Scheme
(vii)	Learning a new language
(viii)	The dangers of the job

Example   SECTION 1

Answer   *V*

---

1.   SECTION 2
2.   SECTION 3
3.   SECTION 4
4.   SECTION 5

The Dams that Changed Australia

Section 1

Inland Australia has had a problem with drought from the time of white settlement in 1788 until today, and this is why the Snowy Mountains Scheme was conceived and founded. Before the Snowy Scheme a large proportion of the snow-fields on the roof of Australia melted into the Snowy River every year, and the water flowed into the sea, not into the dry interior where people needed it so desperately. This was first recognised by the Polish geologist and explorer Strezlecki in 1840, who commented that there could be no development of the inland without irrigation. The rivers would have to be diverted if irrigation were to succeed.

Before Federation in 1901, Australia consisted of a group of colonies, all anxious to protect their own interests. After Federation the states retained rights to the water, and thus to what might happen to the rivers. Arguments between New South Wales, Victoria and South Australia led to a deadlocked Premiers' Conference in 1947. Despite this serious dispute the Federal Parliament passed the Snowy Mountains Hydro-electric Power Act just two years later, on July 7. The project was officially commenced on October 17 that year, barely three months after the Act had been passed.

The scheme set out to harness water for electricity and to divert it back to the dry inland areas for irrigation. To do this, thousands of kilometres of tunnels had to be drilled through the mountains, and sixteen major dams and seven hydro-electric power stations built over a period of nineteen years. The first of these was Guthega Power Station, commissioned in 1954, and the last, Tumut III.

Section 2

The Snowy Mountains Scheme was to alter the face of Australia forever. One important change was the recruitment of people from outside Australia to work on the scheme. In 1949, while the world was still recovering from the effects of World War II (1939 to 1945), the Australian government needed immense numbers of people to work on the Snowy. It sought labour from overseas, and 60,000 of the 100,000 people who worked on the scheme came from outside the country.

They came from thirty different countries: from Italy, Yugoslavia, and Germany, from sophisticated cities like Budapest, Paris and Vienna, and from tiny hamlets. These European workers left countries which had fought against each other during the war, and which had vastly different cultures, and they found themselves in a country which was still defining itself. They were adventurous young men, some highly skilled, some not, and they came to a place which offered both enormous challenges and primitive conditions. Many were housed in tents in the early days of the scheme, although some fortunate men were placed in barracks. The food was basic, female company extremely scarce and entertainment lacking.

Section 3

Many new arrivals spoke only limited English, and were offered English classes after work. The men needed primarily to understand safety instructions, and safety lectures were conducted in English and other languages. In fact a great deal of communication underground was by sign language, especially when the conditions were noisy. The signs were peculiar to the business at hand: for instance, a thumb placed near the mouth meant water, but did not indicate whether the water was needed on the drill the man was using, or for a drink.

The constant reference to the men who worked on the Snowy is appropriate because few women worked on the scheme, and those who were employed usually held office jobs. Women, however, were active in the community, and the members of the Country Women's Association gave English lessons. Other English instruction was provided by The Australian Broadcasting Commission which ran daily broadcasts to help the newcomers with the language.

Section 4

These circumstances could have caused great social trouble, but there were relatively few serious problems. The men worked long and hard, and many saved their money with a view to settling in Australia or returning home. At a reunion in 1999 many were happy to remember the hardships of those days, but it was all seen through a glow of achievement. This satisfaction was felt not only by the men who worked directly on the project, but by the women, many of whom had been wives and mothers during the scheme, and indicated that they had felt very much part of it.

The children of these couples went to school in Happy Jack, a town notable for having the highest school in Australia, and the highest birthrate. In one memorable year there were thirty babies born to the eighty families in Happy Jack. Older children went to school in Cooma, the nearest major town.

Section 5

The scheme is very unlikely to be repeated. The expense of putting the power stations underground would now be prohibitive, and our current information about ecology would require a different approach to the treatment of the rivers. Other hydro-electric schemes like the Tennessee Valley Authority preceded the Snowy Mountains Scheme, and others have followed. The Snowy Mountains Scheme is the only hydro-electric scheme in the world to be totally financed from the sale of its electricity.

As well as being a great engineering feat, the scheme is a monument to people from around the world who dared to change their lives. Some are living and working in Australia, many have retired there, some have returned to their countries of origin. Every one of them contributed to altering Australian society forever.

Questions 5-8

*Complete the table below. Write a date or event for each answer. Use no more than **THREE WORDS OR NUMBERS** for each answer.*

Write your answers in boxes 5-8 on your answer sheet.

	DATE (Year)	EVENT
5		White settlement begins
Example	*1939-1945*	World War II
6		Snowy Mountains Scheme begins
7		Tumut III Power Station commissioned
8	1999	

Questions 9-12

Do the following statements agree with the views of the writer? In boxes 37-40 on your answer sheet write:

YES   *if the statement agrees with the writer*
NO   *if the statement does not agree with the writer*
NOT GIVEN   *if there is no information about this in the passage*

9.   The Snowy Mountains Scheme was designed to meet Australia's energy needs.

10.   Few women played a direct part in the development of the Snowy Mountains Scheme.

11.   The Snowy Mountains Scheme has led to a new set of environmental problems.

12.   The Snowy Mountains Scheme may be considered the beginning of a multicultural Australia.

You should spend about 20 minutes on Questions 13-26 which are based on Reading Passage 2.

Power from the Earth

A. Geothermal power refers to the generation of electrical power from the tapping of heat sources found well below the earth's surface. As most people know, if a hole were to be drilled deep into the earth, extremely hot, molten rock would soon be encountered. At depths of 30 to 50 km, temperatures exceeding 1000 degrees Celsius prevail. Obviously, accessing such temperatures would provide a wonderful source for geothermal power. The problem is, such depths are too difficult to access - drilling down some 30 or more kilometers is simply too costly with today's technology.

B. Fortunately, sufficiently hot temperatures are available at considerably shallower depths. In certain areas, where the earth's surface has been altered over time - through, for example, volcanic activity - temperatures exceeding 300 degrees Celsius can be found at depths of a mere 1 to 3 km, which can be feasibly accessed. These particular areas are potentially ideal for the generation of electricity through geothermal means.

C. It is possible to explain geothermal power generation as a steam power system that utilizes the earth itself as a boiler. When water is sent down to the depths of 1 to 3 km, it returns to the surface as steam and is capable of generating electricity. Electricity generated in this manner hardly produces any carbon dioxide or other waste materials. If the steam and hot water are routed back underground, the generation of electricity can be semipermanent in nature.

D. Furthermore, geothermal power can provide a stable supply of electricity unlike other natural energy sources such as solar power and wind power, which both rely heavily on weather conditions. Accordingly, the generation of electricity through geothermal power is four to five times more efficient than through solar power. As for wind power, geothermal power is some two times more cost effective. Only the generation of hydroelectric power comes close - the cost of power production from each is about the same.

E. Although geothermal power generation appears to be a most attractive option, development has been slow. The world's first successful attempt at geothermal power generation was accomplished in Italy in 1904. Power generation in Japan first started in 1925 at Beppu City. Since that time, countries as diverse as Iceland and New Zealand have joined the list of nations tapping this valuable source of energy. In the year 2000, Beppu City hosted the World Geothermal Congress, whose goal was to promote the adoption of geothermal energy production throughout the world.

F. The international geothermal community at the World Geothermal Congress 2000 called upon the governments of nations to make strong commitments to the development of their indigenous geothermal resources for the benefit of their own people, humanity, and the environment. However, several factors are still hindering the development of geothermal power generation. Firstly, it has a low density of energy which makes it unsuitable for large-scale production in which, for example, over 1 million kilowatts need to be produced. Secondly, the cost is still high when compared to today's most common sources of energy production: fossil fuels and atomic energy.

G. A further consideration is the amount of risk involved in successfully setting up a new geothermal power production facility. The drilling that must extend 2,000 to 3,000 m below the surface must be accurate to within a matter of just a few meters one side or the other of the targeted location. To achieve this, extensive surveys, drilling expertise and time are needed. It is not uncommon for a project to encompass ten years from its planning stage to the start of operations. The extent of the risks involved is clear.

H. Although it has long been considered a resource-poor nation, Japan, which is thought to have about 10% of the world's geothermal resources, may well have considerable advantages for tapping into geothermal power. It does have one of the longest serving power stations using geothermal energy. The station, built in 1966, pointed the way to the future when the country was affected by the two global oil shocks in the 1970s. Now there are some 17 plants in operation throughout the country which are responsible for a total output of over 530,000 kilowatts. This figure, though impressive, accounts for a mere 0.4% of Japan's total generation of electricity.

I. Clearly then, further progress needs to be made in the development of geothermal energy. As long as costs remain high in comparison to other sources of energy, geothermal power will struggle to match the efficiency of existing power sources. Further research and innovation in the field, as well as government support and a sense of urgency, are needed to help propel geothermal energy towards its promising future.

Questions 13-18

Reading Passage 2 has 9 paragraphs labelled A-I.

Which paragraphs contain the following information?

Write the appropriate letters A-I in boxes 13 to 18 on your answer sheet.

13. History of the development of geothermal power

14. One country's use of geothermal power

15. Comparisons between various energy sources

16. How geothermal energy can produce electricity

17. Conditions which permit access to geothermal power

18. Problems of geothermal exploration

Questions 19-26

Do the following statements agree with the information given in the passage "Power from the Earth"?

In boxes 19-26 on your answer sheet write

YES	*if the statement agrees with the writer*
NO	*if the statement does not agree with the writer*
NOT GIVEN	*if there is no information about this in the passage*

19. Accessing geothermal energy at depths greater than 3 km is currently not possible.

20. Geothermal power is unlikely to be economically sensible while carbon fuel is available.

21. The generation of geothermal power does produce some byproducts damaging to the environment.

22. The World Geothermal Congress has been able to raise money for research in this area.

23. Geothermal energy is still relatively expensive to generate.

24. It can take a decade to develop a single geothermal power station.

25. Japan will soon be capable of generating one quarter of its energy needs using geothermal energy.

26. The future of geothermal energy depends upon the decline of fossil fuel resources.

Reading Passage 3

You should spend about 20 minutes on Questions 27-40 which are based on Reading Passage 3.

Are we Managing to Destroy Science?

[The government in UK was concerned about the efficiency of Research institutions and set up a Research Assessment Exercise (RAE) to consider what was being done in each university. The article which follows is a response to the imposition of the RAE.]

MICHAEL J LARKIN

In the year ahead, the UK government is due to carry out the next Research Assessment Exercise (RAE). The goal of this regular five-yearly check up of the university sector is easy to understand - perfection, of a kind, in public sector research. But perfection extracts a high price. In the case of the RAE, one risk attached to this is the creation of a tyrannical management culture that threatens the future of imaginative science.

Academic institutions are already preparing for the RAE with some anxiety - understandably so, for the financial consequences of failure are severe. Departments with a current rating of four or five (research is rated on a five point scale, with five the highest) must maintain their score or face a considerable loss of funding. Meanwhile, those with ratings of two or three are fighting for their survival.

The pressures are forcing research management onto the defensive. Common strategies for increasing academic output include grading individual researchers every year according to RAE criteria, pressurising them to publish anything regardless of quality, diverting funds from key and expensive laboratory science into areas of study such as management, and even threatening to close departments. Another strategy being readily adopted is to remove scientists who appear to be less active in research and replace them with new, probably younger, staff.

Although such measures may deliver results in the RAE, they are putting unsustainable pressure on academic staff. Particularly insidious is the pressure to publish. Put simply, RAE committees in the laboratory sciences must produce four excellent peer-reviewed publications per member of staff to meet the assessment criteria. Hence this is becoming a minimum requirement for existing members of staff, and a benchmark against which to measure new recruits.

But prolific publication does not necessarily add up to good science. Indeed, one young researcher was told in an interview for a lectureship that, "although your publications are excellent unfortunately there are not enough of them. You should not worry so much about the quality of your publications."

In a recent letter to *Nature* I analysed the publication records of ten senior academics in the area of molecular microbiology. All of them are now in very senior positions in universities or research institutes, with careers spanning a total of 262 years. All have achieved considerable status and respect within the UK and worldwide. However, their early publication records would preclude them from academic posts if the present criteria were applied.

Although the quality of their work was clearly outstanding - they initiated novel and perhaps risky projects early in their careers which have since been recognised as research of international importance - they generally produced few papers over the first ten years after completing their PhDs. Indeed, over this period, they have an average gap of 3.8 years without publication or production of a cited paper. In one case there was a five-year gap. Although these enquiries were limited to my own area of research, it seems that this model of career progression is widespread in all of the chemical and biological sciences.

It seems that the atmosphere surrounding the RAE may be stifling talented young researchers or driving them out of science altogether. We urgently need a more considered and careful nurturing of our young scientific talent. A new member of academic staff in the chemical or biological laboratory sciences surely needs a commitment to resources over a five- to ten-year period to establish their research. Senior academics managing this situation might be well advised to demand a long-term view from the government.

Unfortunately, management seems to be pulling in the opposite direction. Academics have to deal with more students than ever and the paperwork associated with teaching quality assessments is increasing. On top of that, the salary for university lecturers starts at only £16,665 (rising to £29,048). Tenure is rare, and most contracts are offered on a temporary contract basis. With the mean starting salary for new graduates now close to £18,000, it is surprising that anybody still wants a job in academia.

It need not be like this. As part of my duties with the QUESTOR Centre (Queen's University Environmental Science and Technology Research Centre), I have dealings with many senior research managers in the chemical and water industries. The overall impression is that the private sector has a much more sensible and enlightened long-term view of research priorities. Why can the universities not develop the same attitude?

Tyrannies need managers, and these managers will make sure they survive when those they manage are lost. Research management in UK universities is in danger of evolving into such a tyranny that it will allow little time for careful thinking and teaching, and will undermine the development of imaginative young scientists.

Dr Larkin is a senior lecturer in microbiology at The Queen's University Belfast.

Questions 27-34

*Complete the summary below. Choose **NO MORE THAN ONE WORD** from the box below for each answer, and write them in boxes 27-34 on your answer sheet.*

> rated   academic   publish   carried   business
>
> disagree   worried   strict   excited   scientific   conducted
>
> negotiate   counterproductive   published   expensive
>
> retrain   complex   abstract   popular   replace

The next Research Assessment Exercise (RAE) is due to be ____(27)____ next year. Already, universities in the UK are ____(28)____ about the exercise. It involves individual departments being ____(29)____ for their ability to measure up to specified criteria. The purpose of the exercise is to increase ____(30)____ output, yet the author considers the exercise to be counterproductive.

To meet the ____(31)____ criteria, some departments will force their staff to ____(32)____ anything. Others may reallocate funds toward subjects that are less ____(33)____ than laboratory science. One further approach is to ____(34)____ existing staff.

Question 35-40

Do the following statements agree with the views of the writer in Reading Passage 3?
In boxes 35-40 on your answer sheet write:

YES	*if the statement agrees with the writer*
NO	*if the statement does not agree with the writer*
NOT GIVEN	*if there is no information about this in the passage*

35. The current management of research projects is unlikely to produce good science.

36. Good researchers are usually good teachers.

37. Good researchers are usually prolific publishers.

38. People in industry seem to understand the long-term nature of research.

39. We can hope for more exciting research under the influence of industry.

40. Managers/management may be the only winners under the new system.

Unit 4
The Writing test

How to use this Unit

This Unit contains:

- Global strategies for the Academic Module Writing tasks. These strategies will show you how to analyse the Writing Tasks, and what you must do to give a satisfactory answer.

- 5 Academic Writing Practice Tests. Each has two Writing Tasks similar to the kind of tasks found in the real IELTS test. To do these practice tests under exam conditions, you must complete each test in 1 hour. Keep to the suggested time of 20 minutes for Writing Task 1 and 40 minutes for Writing Task 2. Sit in a quiet place where you will not be disturbed, and DO NOT use a dictionary.

Global Strategies for the Academic Module Writing Tasks

The Academic Writing Test is challenging. In one hour you must complete two complex tasks, of different kinds, both of which require advanced language skills.

This section describes the two writing tasks required for the examination, and indicates what the examiner is looking for. This is followed by five Practice Tests. Suggested approaches to the tasks in the Practice Tests are provided in the Answer Key. Please do not read these until you have attempted the tasks. Remember that these are suggestions only and that your answers may be equally valid. It is valuable to discuss your answers with other students.

The Tasks
For the Academic Writing Module you are required to answer two tasks, of different types and lengths. Some of these differences are summarised below.

	Task 1	**Task 2**
Suggested Time	20 minutes	40 minutes
Length	150+ words	250+ words
Paragraphs	1-2	4 or more
Introduction	1 sentence	1 paragraph
Conclusion	1-2 sentences	1-2 paragraphs
Function	Describe: • data • procedures • objects • a series of events	Convince by: • giving reasons, examples • comparing • weighing up advantages and disadvantages

The word length for both tasks should be taken seriously; if your answer is too short, you will lose marks.

We will now look at each task in more detail.

Writing Task 1

The task
Task 1 requires a **description** of a graph, table, flowchart or diagram. You are not required to give an opinion about the information presented, simply to use sentences to describe what is presented in numeric or diagrammatic form.

Analysing the question
To be sure that you answer the question correctly, follow these steps:

1. Read the heading of the diagram, and note the vocabulary (it will be useful in your answer). What is the **topic** of the graph(s)/diagrams?

2. Determine the **dimensions** in the diagram (what kinds of measurements are being used: percentages, money, time, number of people, etc.).

3. (a) For graphs/tables: sometimes the task will contain a great deal of information. It is not usually necessary to mention every number. Instead, think about the following questions:

   - What are the most striking features of the graphs?
   - Are there general trends (eg. gradual increases or decreases)?
   - Are there points of comparison or points of contrast?

   Use these ideas as the basis for your answer.

   (b) For processes: unlike graphs and tables, you will need to describe everything that is labelled in the diagram. For flowcharts, organise your answer to follow the sequence outlined in the chart.

What the examiner is looking for

A simple writing structure. The examiner will mainly be looking to see how well you can use the language of description, so you do not need to write a long and elaborate introduction or conclusion. Your answer may have the following basic structure:

1. A short opening sentence to describe the topic of the diagram, followed by ...
2. Several paragraphs describing the steps in the process/ information shown in the graph, and then ...
3. A closing sentence or two commenting on one or two interesting features of the graph.

A variety of sentence structures. Read the following segment, which is taken from a student's answer to a Task 1 question:

> *The number of people drinking coffee went up to 2 mil in 1990. Then it went up to 2.2 mil in 1991. Then it went down to 1.8 mil in 1992 ...*

An answer like this that continues on in the same way, using the same sentence structure all the time, is not acceptable. If you continue to use the same sentence patterns all the way through your answer, it will become very boring. Also you will not show the examiner the full extent of your language ability, so you will not get all the marks you deserve.

Effective use of vocabulary. The examiner will want to see how well you can use the vocabulary found in the diagram(s). To use it effectively in your answer will sometimes mean that you have to change a noun in the diagram to a verb to fit into your sentence. You can find out about word families (word formation) in English from a textbook. Practise changing words from nouns to verbs (and so on) in preparation for the test.

Writing Task 2

The Task

For this task students are required to answer a question convincingly by presenting evidence (reasons) for their point of view. The answer should be in the form of an academic essay. Sometimes your essay will have to argue for a single point of view, sometimes it will have to compare and evaluate opposing points of view, and sometimes it will have to present a solution to a problem. In all these different essay types you will be required to give evidence for your point of view.

Analysing the question

The format of the question may vary widely. The question may be prefaced by several sentences which provide a background to the topic, or give examples. On the other hand, the question may appear as a statement, with which you must agree or disagree, or even as a group of related questions.

Part of the mark given for your essay depends on how well you answer the question, so take time to read the question carefully, to make your answer as suitable as possible.

1. As with Task 1, your first step must be to determine the **topic** of the question. Start by identifying the key words in the question. If the question is short, the topic will be easy to find. If the question is in the shape of a long paragraph, try looking towards the end to find the main ideas.

2. Determine the **task**. Now that you know the topic of the essay, you need to know in what way you must discuss it.

    *   Are you required to present a solution?
    *   Are you required to present an opinion?
    *   Are you required to evaluate (or compare) opposing opinions?
        (this question will often be in the form of *To what extent ...*)

Once you have determined the task, you can begin to plan your answer.

3. Use ideas in the whole question to assist you. Although a long question can be difficult when determining the topic and task, it can be useful when planning the structure of your essay. It will usually contain examples and ideas that you can discuss in your essay, although you will also need to provide more examples and ideas of your own.

Your Plan

It is absolutely essential for your essay that you read the question carefully, and plan your essay. It is worth using precious time - 5-10 minutes out of the 40 minutes suggested - to carefully analyse the question, think of ideas, then organise them, so that you are ready to write. There are several advantages to doing this:

*   by reading the question slowly and carefully you will make your answer more relevant and gain more marks

- by brainstorming and planning, you will be able to think of the best ideas. You will not run out of ideas and repeat the same points over and over again
- your answer will be well structured, because you have thought about the structure before you started writing
- you will be able to concentrate on writing your ideas clearly and with grammatical accuracy, and not be trying to think of what to write next. You will be able to concentrate on *how* to write, not *what* to write.

A plan does not have to be complicated, but it should contain:

- a note of your main ideas, and the evidence you will use to support them
- the order in which your ideas will appear
- how these ideas will be separated into paragraphs.

What the examiner is looking for
An academic essay. Your answer to this question should take the form of an academic essay, which contains:

1. an introduction, which presents the question, and outlines the arguments the writer will use;
2. a main section or body, where the ideas are discussed in detail, with evidence to support these ideas;
3. a conclusion, in which a final decision is reached, and the writer makes clear which ideas are the most important.

The exact organisation of your essay will depend on the specific Writing Task you have to do.

Evidence. One of the main problems students have is that they do not present enough detail in their essays. For every idea that you put in your essay, you must prove to your reader why it is so. Presenting evidence and examples to back up your claims will also help you achieve your desired word length.

This section has given a brief overview of the task types used in the Academic Writing Module, and some suggestions to help you write acceptable answers. However, to do well in this module you will also need more detailed work, particularly on writing essays. Academic writing in English is different to less formal varieties of writing, and quite different to spoken English. To develop your writing skills, you should work through one of the many excellent textbooks on academic writing. This will explain the important aspects of academic writing, and give you assistance in developing the necessary skills.

Academic Writing Practice Test 1

Writing Task 1

You should spend about 20 minutes on this task.

> *The graphs below show the post-school qualifications held*
> *by Australians in the age groups 25 to 34 and 55 to 69.*
>
> *Write a report for a university lecturer describing the information*
> *shown below.*

You should write at least 150 words.

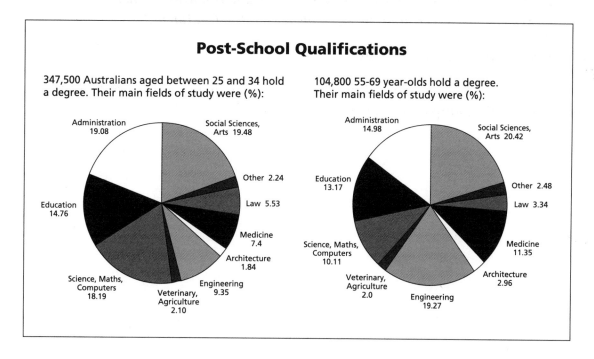

Post-School Qualifications

347,500 Australians aged between 25 and 34 hold a degree. Their main fields of study were (%):

- Administration 19.08
- Social Sciences, Arts 19.48
- Other 2.24
- Law 5.53
- Medicine 7.4
- Architecture 1.84
- Engineering 9.35
- Veterinary, Agriculture 2.10
- Science, Maths, Computers 18.19
- Education 14.76

104,800 55-69 year-olds hold a degree. Their main fields of study were (%):

- Administration 14.98
- Social Sciences, Arts 20.42
- Other 2.48
- Law 3.34
- Medicine 11.35
- Architecture 2.96
- Engineering 19.27
- Veterinary, Agriculture 2.0
- Science, Maths, Computers 10.11
- Education 13.17

Source: *Labour Force Status and Educational Attainment Australia. ABS Cat. No. 6235.0, 1991.*

[Turn over]

Writing Task 2

You should spend about 40 minutes on this task.

Present a written argument or case to an educated non-specialist audience on the following topic.

> *A number of different medical traditions are now widely known and used: Western medicine (using drugs and surgery), herbal medicine, acupuncture (using needles at certain points of the body), homoeopathy (using minute doses of poisons), and so on.*
>
> *How important is the patient's mental attitude towards his/her treatment in determining the effectiveness of the treatment?*

You should write at least 250 words.

You should use your own ideas, knowledge and experience and support your arguments with examples and relevant evidence.

Academic Writing Practice Test 2

Writing Task 1

You should spend about 20 minutes on this task.

> *The following diagram shows nitrogen sources and concentration levels in the groundwater of a coastal city.*
>
> *Write a report for a university lecturer describing the information shown below.*

You should write at least 150 words.

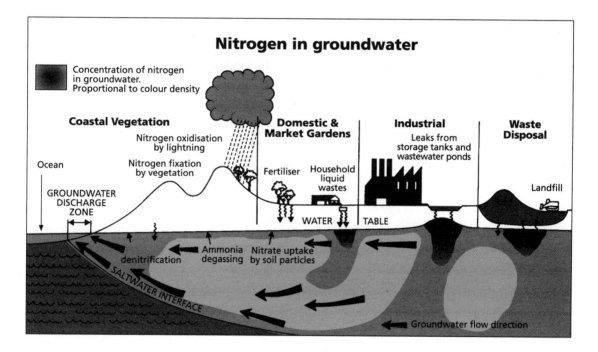

[Turn over]

Writing Task 2

You should spend about 40 minutes on this task.

Present a written argument or case to an educated non-specialist audience on the following topic.

> *A government's role is only to provide defence capability and urban infrastructure (roads, water supplies, etc.). All other services (education, health, social security) should be provided by private groups or individuals in the community.*
>
> *To what extent do you agree or disagree with this opinion?*

You should write at least 250 words.

You should use your own ideas, knowledge and experience and support your arguments with examples and relevant evidence.

Academic Writing Practice Test 3

Writing Task 1

You should spend about 20 minutes on this task.

> *The following graphs give information about the Gross Domestic Product (GDP) and employment sectors of a developing country.*
>
> *Write a report for a university lecturer describing the information shown below.*

You should write at least 150 words.

Sectoral distribution of employment and GDP, 1992

	Natural Resources %	Industry %	Trade, restaurants, hotels %	Transport communication %	Government %	Other %	Total %
			services				
Employment	77.4	3.6	4.9	1.6	8.7	3.8	100.00
GDP	19.2	15.4	37.1	8.4	12.5	7.4	100.00

Percentage of GDP

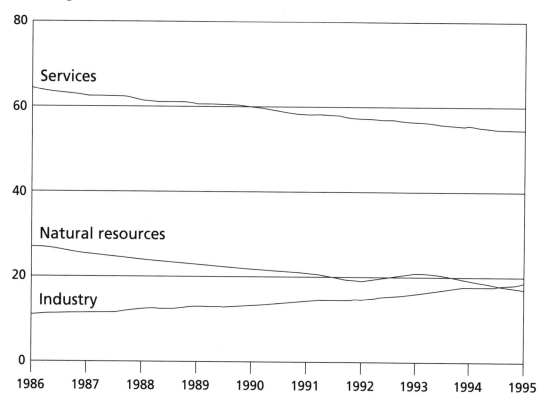

[Turn over]

Writing Task 2

You should spend about 40 minutes on this task.

Present a written argument or case to an educated non-specialist audience on the following topic:

> *Are computers an essential feature of modern education? What subjects can be better taught using computers? Are there aspects of a good education that cannot be taught using computers?*

You should write at least 250 words.

You should use your own ideas, knowledge and experience and support your arguments with examples and relevant evidence.

Academic Writing Practice Test 4

Writing Task 1

You should spend about 20 minutes on this task.

The table below shows consumer preferences for the features of automatic washing machines in different countries.

Write a report for a university lecturer describing the information shown below.

You should write at least 150 words.

Exhibit 1. Consumer preferences as to automatic washing machine features, by country

Features	United Kingdom	Germany	France	Sweden
Shell dimensions (ht. & width)	34" & narrow	34" & wide	34" & narrow	34" & wide
Drum material	Enamel	Stainless steel	Enamel	Stainless steel
Loading	Top	Front	Front	Front
Capacity	5 kilos	6 kilos	5 kilos	6 kilos
Spin speed	700 rpm	850 rps	600 rpm	800 rpm
Water heating system	No	Yes	Yes	No
Styling features	Inconspicuous appearance	Indestructible appearance	Elegant appearance	Strong appearance
Washing action	Agitator	Tumble	Agitator	Tumble

Reprinted by permission of Harvard Business Review [an exhibit]. From "The Globalization of Markets" by T. Levitt, May/June 1983. Copyright © by the President and Fellows of Harvard College; all rights reserved.

[Turn over]

Writing Task 2

You should spend about 40 minutes on this task.

Present a written argument or case to an educated non-specialist audience on the following topic.

> *The private motor vehicle has greatly improved individual freedom of movement. Moreover, the automobile has become a status symbol. Yet the use of private motor vehicles has contributed to some of today's most serious problems.*
>
> *How can the use of private motor vehicles be reduced?*

You should write at least 250 words.

You should use your own ideas, knowledge and experience and support your arguments with examples and relevant evidence.

Academic Writing Practice Test 5

Writing task 1

You should spend about 20 minutes on this task.

> *The graphs below show the enrolments of overseas students and local students in Australian universities between 1989 and 1999.*
>
> *Write a report for a university lecturer describing the information shown below.*

You should write at least 150 words.

Enrolments 1989-1999

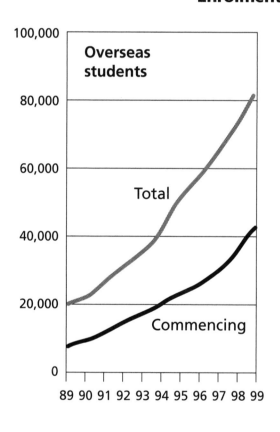
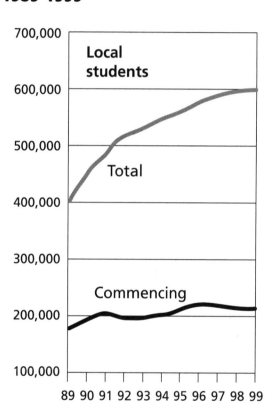

[Turn over]

Writing Task 2

You should spend about 40 minutes on this task.

Present a written argument or case to an educated reader with no specialist knowledge of the following topic.

> *Some people say that universities should be concerned with educating people so that they will have wide general knowledge and be able to consider important matters from an informed viewpoint. Other people say that universities should simply train students to do the jobs required by society, and not concern themselves with broader issues.*
>
> *What do you think?*

You should write at least 250 words.

You should use your own ideas, knowledge and experience and support your arguments with examples and relevant evidence.

Unit 5
The Speaking test

How to use this Unit

This Unit contains:

- An introduction to the new IELTS Speaking test.

- A description of the three parts of the IELTS interview and suggestions on how to prepare for each part, including practice topics.

Information and strategies for the new Speaking test

Description of the Speaking test

The Speaking test consists of an oral interview between you, the candidate, and an examiner. It will last between 11 and 14 minutes, and is divided into three parts which are described below.

The aim of the test is to assess the candidate's ability to communicate effectively in English, and the examiner will consider your: Fluency and Coherence; Lexical Resource: Grammatical Range and Accuracy; and Pronunciation.

These criteria will be discussed below.

Revision of the IELTS Speaking Test in 2001
Introduction to the IELTS Interview

Like the Listening test, the Speaking test is taken by all candidates, whether they are taking the Academic or General Training modules. It is a one-to-one interview of 11 to 14 minutes and may be done on the day of the examination, or up to two days later, at the discretion of the examination centre.

Your examiner is a qualified teacher who has been appointed by the test centre and approved by the British Council or IELTS Australia. He or she is likely to be very experienced in dealing with students.

There are three main parts to the interview. The examiner has been trained to guide candidates through the interview, and will help you to feel comfortable. The interview will be recorded.

The examiner will have to follow a script, or frame, during the interview. This frame means that everyone doing the Speaking test will receive the same instructions and information in the same manner. Your examiner will be more constrained in Part 1 and Part 2 of the test. In Part 3, the two-way discussion, the examiner will have a less restrictive frame, but will still have very firm rules to follow.

Description of the three parts of the interview

Part 1
In this part you will answer general questions. The examiner will ask you about things which are close to you and which should be easy for you to answer. The examiner may ask you about yourself, your home and your family, what sort of job you have, what you are studying, or he or she may want to know about your particular interests. This part will last between four and five minutes.

Part 2
In Part 2 the examiner will give you a verbal prompt on a card and will ask you to talk on a particular topic. You will have one minute to prepare your answer before speaking at length for between one or two minutes. After you have spoken the examiner will ask some questions which arise from what you have said. These questions will bring Part 2 to a conclusion. The whole of Part 2 lasts between three and four minutes, which includes the one minute spent preparing the answer.

Part 3
In Part 3 the examiner will get you to develop the ideas on the topic you have been discussing in Part 2. The discussion will continue between four and five minutes.

How to approach the test

Part 1
The examiner will introduce him or herself and ask for your identification. The examiner may also ask you how to pronounce your name correctly.

This part of the interview takes four to five minutes, and should allow you to settle down and feel comfortable.

Part I is concerned with familiar topics of general interest.

Preparing for Part 1
Make sure you know the English vocabulary you might use to speak about familiar topics, so you can talk about topics like your home, your family, your course of study or your job. It is a good idea to think about the sort of things your examiner might ask you about. If you are studying with other students, be ready to question each other about your homes and families, jobs and studies and your interests.

You will notice that it is a very wide list, and it is impossible to guess the specific topic you will be asked to discuss. If, for instance, your examiner wants you to talk about your interests, he or she might ask you what sport/hobby/pastime you are interested in, and when, where and why you became interested. Or he or she might ask if that particular hobby is popular in your country, or if your parents share your interest, or if your hobby is expensive …

Please do not think you can prepare a talk on any topic and take it into the examination. The examiner will be in control of the interaction, and may prompt you with questions or change the direction of the conversation. The examiner will not permit a prepared speech.

Develop the topic as fully as you can, and offer your own ideas and give explanations if necessary. Do not simply answer "Yes" or "No" to the examiner's questions.

If possible, practise asking and answering questions with another person. Do not let the person you are talking to correct you or prompt you while you are speaking. If you want to be corrected, record your conversation and then listen to it and see how you might improve it.

Part 2
In Part 2 the candidate is given a verbal prompt on a card and is asked to talk on a particular topic. The candidate has one minute to prepare before speaking at length, for between one or two minutes. The examiner then asks one or two follow-up questions.

Describe the thing you most like to do when you have some free time.

　　You should say:

　　　　what it is
　　　　what you do
　　　　what makes you enjoy the activity

　　and explain why this activity is important to you.

You will have to talk about this topic for one to two minutes.
You have one minute to think about what you are going to say.
You can make some notes to help you if you wish.

Preparing for Part 2
It is a good idea to practise talking on a topic for one or two minutes, and to practise making notes to help you. Do not write too much, and do not allow more than one minute for preparation time.

Practise with the topic above. The first instruction is to *Describe* the thing you most like to do when you have some free time.

What do you like to do? When you describe something, you say what it is, and you should you make a word picture which tells the listener about what you like to do in your free time. For example, you might like to go to the movies. Describe

---

the sort of movies you enjoy, and when you get to see them. Maybe you have favourite actors. You might talk about them. Describe the sort of movie theatre you like to visit, and how you get there. You could talk about who you go with, and what you both enjoy, or whether you have differing tastes.

After that, you should explain why going to the movies is important to you. Think of reasons. It could be because you like to be able to talk to other people about what you have seen, or you enjoy having stories told to you, or you think that movies are an important part of our culture. Explain your reasons as fully as you can.

Your examiner will ask you some questions just to round off the topic. If you talk about a particular actor your examiner might ask if you know something more about him or her. Or you might be asked more about the movie theatre you attend, and why you go there.

Here is another topic you might like to practise:

> **Tell the examiner about your favourite festival.**
>
> **You should say:**
>
> > **where it is**
> >
> > **what it is celebrating**
> >
> > **what makes you enjoy the things that happen**
>
> **and explain why this festival is important to you.**

Your examiner will ask you some questions about the festival you have chosen.

Time yourself making notes for up to a minute and talking for a minute or two. Talk on any topic you know well. It is a good idea to use a timer, and a small piece of paper so you cannot write too much. Your prompts should only be one or two words long.

It is also a good idea to record yourself and then play back the recording so you can think of ways you could improve your talk. Here are some questions you could ask yourself:

- Did I answer the question?
- Did I give enough details?
- Could I develop the ideas more?
- Did I keep using the same vocabulary? What other words could I use?
- Was my grammar correct?
- Was my pronunciation clear?
- How could I make my notes more helpful?
- Did I talk for at least one minute? Did I take more than two minutes?

Timing is important. You must speak for at least one minute so the examiner can get a good sample of your speaking to listen to. On the other hand, if you take more than two minutes in the examination, the examiner will have to stop you so you can go on with the rest of the Speaking Test. Do not be upset by this. The test has to be fitted into the 14 minutes allotted, so the examiner cannot let you go on over time.

Part 3

In Part 3 the examiner and candidate develop the discussion which began in Part 2. The discussion lasts between four and five minutes. The examiner will get the candidate to enlarge upon things which were discussed in the second part of the test.

Preparing for Part 3

Practise discussing topics at length with another person. For instance, take a topic which you have discussed in level 2 and enlarge upon it. If possible, work with another person and take it in turns to be examiner and candidate. The person playing the role of examiner should ask questions and give the person playing the part of the candidate plenty of time to answer. Perhaps you have been talking about entertainment where you live. You should be ready to talk about other possibilities: what if your favourite movie house closed down? Do you feel disillusioned with the behaviour of some of the actors? How do you think the pressure of fame can be managed?

Factors in your assessment:

Candidates are assessed on Fluency and Coherence; Lexical Resource; Grammatical Range and Accuracy; and Pronunciation.

Fluency is the quality of being able to speak without too many pauses and hesitations.

Coherence refers to the way you stay on the topic and argue it clearly, so the listener can follow your ideas easily.

Lexical Resource refers to your use of words, the range and accuracy of your vocabulary and how well you use it. You should keep in mind that this is a fairly formal situation, and your language and your manner should not be too casual.

Grammatical Range and Accuracy refers to the number of grammatical forms which you can use, and how well you can use them. It is better to be able to use many different constructions, and not to be limited to subject/verb/object sentences like *The cat caught a rat*. Accuracy refers to the appropriate use of language, for instance correctly using the different tenses of English.

Pronunciation refers to whole sentences and not just single words. It is important that the examiner is able to understand what you are saying. You are not expected to sound like a native speaker of English.

The examiner will assess you on each of these factors and will give you an overall Bandscore of 1 to 9. Bandscores were discussed in Unit 1.

How you can help yourself to do well

Practise speaking English with your friends. If they are preparing for the IELTS test you might like to interview each other. If you are talking with people who are not studying for the IELTS test, the practice you get in using English will be valuable.

You might like to taperecord your conversations and listen to them again later. It is better to consider how you could improve your grammar and pronunciation after you have listened to the tape; if you worry about your grammar while you are speaking you will be less fluent. It is better not to let people correct you **while** you are speaking, but to wait until you have finished speaking.

During the examination, the examiner will guide you. The examiner has to keep control of the progress and timing of the different parts of the interview and so you should take your cues from him/her. Answer the questions as well as you can, and remember the examiner is there to help you achieve your best level.

Finally, please remember this is a speaking test, and the only way to prepare for it is to speak.

Unit 6
Answers and tapescripts

The reading, writing and listening practice tests in this book have been designed to resemble the format of the IELTS test as closely as possible. They are not, however, real IELTS tests; they simply give practice in the type of question students may have to answer in the real test. For this reason, there is no system of marking or scoring the practice tests in this book, so the tests cannot be used to assess or predict band scores. These practice tests are designed to practise exam technique to help students to face the IELTS test with confidence and to perform to the best of their ability.

Part 1: Academic Practice Listening Tests

Cassette 1 Side A

Narrator: Here are some instructions regarding these Practice Listening Tests. In each Practice Listening Test on these two tapes you will hear a number of different recordings, and you will have to answer questions on what you hear. There will be time for you to read the instructions and questions, and you will have a chance to check your work. All the recordings will be played once only.

Each test is in four sections. Write all your answers on the Listening Module Answer sheet. At the end of the real test you will be given ten minutes to transfer your answers to an answer sheet.

Academic Practice Listening Test 1

Answer Key: Academic Practice Listening Test 1

Section 1 Questions 1-12	Section 2 Questions 13-24	Section 3 Questions 25-36	Section 4 Questions 37-41
1. 10 Bridge Street	13. garbage	25. Spanish	37. ✓ *lines for* London, New York, Sydney, Paris, Tokyo *(All ticked= 1 mark, fewer or more = 0; some right/wrong = 0)*
2. writing / writing class	14. garbage	26. Building A	
3. Mrs Green	15. garbage	27. 6 pm	
4. July 15(th) / 15(th) July / 15/7	16. paper	28. Elementary 1 / one	
5. 1 / one	17. charity	29. August 10(th) / 10(th) August / 10/8	38. ✓ *lines for* London, Hong Kong, New York, Sydney, Paris *(All ticked= 1 mark, fewer or more = 0; some right/wrong = 0)*
6. May 31(st) / 31(st) May / 31/5	18. filters	30. D	
7. June 4(th) / 4(th) June / 6/4	19. A	31. C	
8. 3 / three (days)	20. B	32. D	39. (very) / (extremely) poor
9. A	21. D	33. A	40. at different times
10. C	22. B	34. D	41. special (driving / priority) lanes
11. B	23. D	35. F	
12. B	24. C	36. G	

Tapescript: Listening Practice Test 1

Cassette 1 Side A

Narrator: Here are some instructions regarding these Practice Listening Tests. In each Practice Listening Test on these two tapes you will hear a number of different recordings, and you will have to answer questions on what you hear. There will be time for you to read the instructions and questions, and you will have a chance to check your work. All the recordings will be played once only.

Each test is in four sections. Write all your answers on the Listening Module Answer sheet. At the end of the real test you will be given ten minutes to transfer your answers to an answer sheet.

Prepare for IELTS Practice Listening Tests.This is tape 1. Practice Listening Test 1.Turn to Section 1 of Practice Listening Test 1.

Section 1. Listen to the conversation between Bob Wills, who is a foreign student adviser at a language school, and Angela Tung, who is a student, and complete the form.

First you have some time to look at Questions 1 to 8 on the form now.

You will see that there is an example which has been done for you. The conversation relating to this will be played first.

Telephone rings

Bob: Hello, Foreign Student Adviser's office. This is Bob Wills speaking. Can I help you?

Angela: It's Angela Tung here, Bob. I'd like to make a request for special leave. Can I do that over the phone?

Bob: Hello Angela. You can make that request by phone - but I'll have to fill the form out. Let me get the special leave form. Okay.Here it is. Tell me your student number, please.

Angela: It's H for Harry 5712.

Bob: H 5712. Okay. What's your address, Angela?

Narrator: Angela's student number is H5712, so that has been written on the form. Now we shall begin. You should answer the questions as you listen because you will not hear the recording a second time. Now listen carefully and answer questions 1 to 8.

Telephone rings

Bob: Hello, Foreign Student Adviser's office. This is Bob Wills speaking. Can I help you?

Angela: It's Angela Tung here, Bob. I'd like to make a request for special leave. Can I do that over the phone?

Bob: Hello Angela. You can make that request by phone - but I'll have to fill the form out. Let me get the special leave form. Okay.Here it is. Tell me your student number, please.

Angela: It's H for Harry 5712.

Bob: H 5712. Okay. What's your address, Angela?

Angela: I live at 10 Bridge Street, Tamworth.

Bob: 10 Bridge Street, Tamworth. And your phone number?

Angela: The telephone number's 810 6745.

Bob: Thanks. What course are you doing?

Angela: I'm in the writing class.

Bob: Writing. Who's your teacher this term?

Angela: Mrs Green - she spells her name like the colour.

Bob: Thanks. Hmm. When does your student visa expire?

Angela: Let me look. July 15.

Bob: July 15. Okay. Which term do you want to take leave?

Angela: Do you want dates?

Bob: First, I have to write a term number. When do you want to take leave?

Angela: In term one.

Bob: Okay. Term one. Now can you tell me what are the exact dates?

Angela: I'd like to be away May 31 to June 4.

Bob: Okay. I've got that. You'll miss four working days between May 31 and June 4. Is that right?

Angela: Only three. I'll be away over a weekend. I'll be back at my classes on June 5, so that's three days away.

Narrator: Look at questions 9 to 12.

Now listen to more of the conversation between Angela and Bob, and answer questions 9 to 12.

Bob: Why do you want to take leave, Angela?

Angela: I'm going to visit my aunt May. She's my mother's sister. She and her husband are my guardians while I'm here.

Bob: Where do they live?

Angela: About fifty kilometres from here, near Armidale.

Bob: Do you have to take so long if they live nearby?

Angela: My mother is coming with me. She's come for a holiday, so she wants to have some time with May, and I want to spend some time with my mother, too.

Bob: Aren't you going home soon?

Angela: I've applied to extend my time here. I expect to go home in twelve months.

Narrator: That is the end of Section 1. You now have some time to check your answers.

Now turn to Section 2.

Section 2. You are going to hear a tape recording of instructions and advice which a woman called Martha has left for her friend John, who is coming to stay at her house and take care of it while she is away. First, look at questions 13 to 18.

As you listen to the first part of the talk, answer questions 13 to 18.

Martha: Hello, John. Welcome to the house. I'm really pleased that you can be here to look after my house while I'm away.

Here are some things you need to know about the house. Important stuff like when the garbage is collected. In fact, let's start with the garbage, which is collected on Friday. Just write "Garbage" on the calendar on the days they take it away. Put it out on Friday every week, that'll be Friday 22nd, Friday 29th and Friday 5th. It's a really good service. The trucks are quiet and the service is efficient. The bin will be put back outside the house empty. It's a good idea to put it away quickly. This street can be quite windy. I once watched my next door neighbour chase her bin the whole length of the street. Every time she nearly caught up with it, it got away again. The waste paper will be collected this Tuesday, that's Tuesday 19th. There's a plastic box full of paper in the front room: please put it out on Tuesday. The truck will come during the day. If you don't mind collecting old newspapers and other paper and putting them in the box I'll put it out when I come home - the paper people only come monthly.

I have some things to give to charity in a box in the front room. Would you put it out on Monday the 25th please? It's a box of old clothes and some bed linen which I've collected, plus a few other bits and pieces. Be careful when you pick it up, because it's heavier than you might expect. The charity truck will come by during the day on the last Monday of the month.

If you want to use the library, you'll find it on Darling Street. I've left my borrower's card near the telephone. It has a very good local reference section if you want to find out more about this city.

I'm sorry to say we don't have a cleaner. Oh, yes! Filters! Please would you change the filters on the washing machine on the last day of the month, which is Sunday the 31st. We find that the machine works much better if we change the filters regularly. The gas company reads the meter outside the house, so don't worry about that. I think that's all the information about our calendar of events.

Narrator: Now look at questions 19 to 24. Circle the correct answer.

Martha: Well, John, I'm trying to think what else I should be telling you. As you know, I'm going to a conference in London. I hope to have a little time to look around. It's a great city! I do hope I manage to get to at least some of the theatres and museums. I'm looking forward to all the things I have to do at the conference, too. I'm giving a paper on Tuesday the 26th and there are a couple of really exciting events planned later in the conference program. I hope to meet up with an old teacher of mine at the conference. She taught English Literature at my old high school and we've kept in touch through letters over the years. She teaches now at the University of Durham, and I'm really looking forward to seeing her again.

By the way, I expect you're hungry after your trip. I've left a meal in the refrigerator for you. I hope you like cheese and onion pie.

Would you do me a favour please? I haven't had time to cancel an appointment. It was made a long time ago and I forgot about it until this morning. It's with my dentist, for a check-up on Thursday the 28th. Could you please call the dentist on 816 2525 and cancel the appointment for me? Thanks a lot, John.

One last thing. When you leave the house, make sure the windows and doors are shut, and set the burglar alarm. The alarm code number is 9-1-2-0 enter. Have fun! I'll see you when I get back. This is your friend Martha, saying goodbye.

Narrator: That is the end of Section 2. You will now have some time to check your answers.

Now turn to Section 3.

Section 3. In this section you will hear a discussion between a college receptionist, Denise, and a student named Vijay about learning a language. In the first part of the discussion they are talking about the course Vijay will study. First look at questions 25 to 29. Note

the examples that have been done for you. Using no more than three words or numbers, complete the table.

Denise: Hello. May I help you?

Vijay: Hello. Is this the right place for me to register to study foreign languages?

Denise: Yes, it is. May I have your name please?

Vijay: Vijay. My family name is Paresh.

Denise: Vijay Paresh. Okay. Do you have a telephone number?

Vijay: Yeh. 909 2467.

Denise: Thank you. Now, which language would you like to learn? We offer French, Italian, Cantonese, Mandarin, Spanish, Portugese ...

Vijay: Ah. I'd like to learn Spanish, please.

Denise: Okay. Our classes are conducted in lots of different places. We have classrooms in the city and here in this building ...

Vijay: What's this building called?

Denise: This is Building A.

Vijay: I work near here, so it'd be best to study in Building A.

Denise: What time do you want to to come to lessons? They go on for three hours, and they start at 10.00 am, 4.00 pm and 6.00 pm.

Vijay: I wish I could come to the daytime lessons, but I can't, so 6.00 pm please.

Denise: That's our most popular time, of course. Umm. Have you ever studied Spanish before?

Vijay: No, I haven't.

Denise: We describe our classes by level and number. Your class is called "Elementary One."

Vijay: Okay. When will classes start?

Denise: Elementary One begins - ah - just a minute - ah - it begins on August 10.

Vijay: Great! Now what else do I have to do?

Narrator: Now look at questions 30 to 32. Choose the appropriate letters A to D and write them in boxes 30 to 32 on your answer sheet. Listen carefully to the conversation between Denise and Vijay and Anne.

Denise: Well, let's see. First, you have to go to ...

Anne: May I have a minute please Denise?

Denise: Of course, Anne. Excuse me for a minute, please, Vijay.

Anne: Did you file those forms for me last night?

Denise: Ah. No. They're still on my desk.

Anne: Oh, Denise, that's simply not good enough!

Denise: I'm really sorry, Anne. It won't happen again.

Anne: All right Denise. Go back to your customer. But please be more careful in future.

Narrator: Now listen to the directions and match the places in questions 33 to 36 to the appropriate letters A to H on the plan.

Denise: I'm sorry Vijay. What were you saying?

Vijay: I wanted to know what else I had to do.

Denise: Oh, of course. Please go to the building on the other side of Smith Street. I want you to go to the reception area first. It's just inside the door on the left as you enter from Smith Street. Give them this form.

Vijay: Okay. Do I pay my fees there?

Denise: No, but the fees office is in the same building.

Go past the escalators and you'll see a games shop. It's in the corner. The fees office is between the games shop and the toilets.

Vijay: Thanks. Er. Where can I buy books?

Denise: The bookshop is opposite the lifts. It's right next to the entrance from Robert Street.

Vijay: Your offices are spread out!

Denise: Not as badly as they used to be. By the way, we offer very competitive overseas travel rates to our students.

Vijay: Oh, I'd like to look into that.

Denise: Of course. The travel agency is at the Smith Street end of the building, in the corner next to the insurance office.

Vijay: Thank you very much. Bye.

Narrator: This is the end of Section 3. You will now have some time to check your answers. Now turn to Section 4.

Section 4. You will hear an extract from a lecture on traffic management. Listen to what the speaker says, and answer questions 37 to 41. First you have some time to look at the questions. Now listen carefully and answer questions 37 and 38. Tick all the relevant boxes in each column.

Tom Fisher: Good afternoon. I'm Tom Fisher, and I'll be lecturing you on traffic management this term. Before we go any further, I thought you should look at the sort of problems we've inherited - and "inherited", or received as a legacy from those before us, is just the word for our situation. Many of our major cities were built long before the car was thought of, and the road system evolved from the goat tracks followed by the early inhabitants. These we can refer to as old-structure problems, and you can take the expression "old-structure" to refer to problems which were in place before we saw the need to build efficient road systems.

Old-structure problems are easily demonstrated in London, New York, Sydney and Paris. Let's look at each city in turn. London has a most confusing road system, which is forgiveable because it's a very old city. I'll talk more about the ring roads later. New York is laid out on a grid which makes it easier to find your way around, but it's an enormous city and the sheer pressure of numbers strangles the roads. Sydney has narrow streets in the centre of the city, and the new road works are not keeping up. Paris has wide streets, but it's still the victim of old-structure problems, like Rome and Edinburgh. Tokyo is another city with old-structure problems compounded by a huge population, like New York. Cities which do not have these old-structure problems are Houston, Los Angeles and Dallas. The thing which saves some of these cities is an effective public transport system, usually below ground. London has an old but effective underground train system known as the tube, and a comprehensive bus and train system above ground. Hong Kong has cheap, swift and effective public transport in the form of Mass Transit Railway, buses and ferries. Paris has the Metro underground railway which carries tens of thousands of people daily, and

a large bus system. New York has a comprehensive underground train system, but many people feel that it's dangerous to ride on it - there have been some nasty attacks. However, the trains themselves are efficient, so we have to call it a good system. Sydney has a good public transport system, but only part of it is underground.

Narrator: Now answer questions 39 to 41. Write no more than three words for each answer.

Tom: Notably absent from this discussion of cities with good public transport are the cities I nominated previously as not having old-structure problems: Houston, Los Angeles and Dallas. Let's start with Dallas, a very wealthy city in Texas which has grown up in an era when cars were considered to be essential to move about. It has an excellent road system, as does Houston, another new city with wise city leaders who insisted on good roads. However, the public transport system in both Houston and Dallas is extremely poor. As a result, travel in Dallas and Houston is easy except for peak hour, when a twenty minute run can expand to more than an hour in traffic jams. Los Angeles suffers from chronic highway blockages, despite efforts to encourage people to use public transport.

Cities with good road systems and no old-structure problems can use other methods to reduce the number of vehicles travelling together at peak hour. Flexi-time is one good method: offices open and close at different times so people are travelling to and from work at different times. Vehicles carrying more than one person can use special priority lanes which means they can travel more quickly. There are even systems to make peak hour car use more expensive, with electronic chips recording the presence of a vehicle in a given high traffic area at a given time. So, what can we do? The rest of this course will be devoted to looking at the conflicting demands of road users, and relating the use of the private car to other aspects of the economy. Over the next three weeks we'll be discussing this in more detail ...

Narrator: That is the end of Section 4. You now have some time to check your answers.

That is the end of Listening Practice Test 1.

Answer Key: Academic Practice Listening Test 2

Section 1 Questions 1-10	Section 2 Questions 11-22	Section 3 Questions 23-31	Section 4 Questions 32-40
1. D	11. Mrs Brooks	23. guitar, classical	32. (the) patient / himself
2. A	12. Lee	24. drums , rock	33. smoking
3. C	13. May / Mai / Mei	25. violin, country	34. young men
4. A	14. 002312	26. piano, opera	35. (the) sun
5. (to the/her) office	15. (Mr) Anderson / Andersen	27. flute, jazz	36. public health (standards)
6. (his) brother	16. Flat 5/10 or 5/10 University Avenue / Ave	28. hearts / heartbeat / blood (flow)	37. healthy lifestyle choices
7. (by) 8 pm / 8 o'clock	17. 818 6074	29. blood pressure / heart beat	38. fun / a pleasure
8. City Square	18. B	30. calming / relaxing / gentle	39. warm-up (time) / stretching (exercises)
9. People are funny	19. C	31. cultures	40. cross training
10. (the) new office) / Newtown / New Town	20. B		
	21. D		
	22. C		

Tapescript: Practice Listening Test 2

Cassette 1 Side A Listening Test 2 Sections 1, 2 and 3. Section 4 is on Cassette 1, Side B
Narrator: Prepare for IELTS Practice Listening Tests.Practice Listening Test 2.
Turn to Section 1 of Practice Listening Test 2.
Section 1. This conversation is between two people, Tom and Mary, who are choosing radios, televisions and telephones in an electronics shop. Listen to the conversation and decide which of the items in the picture, A, B, C, or D they are going to buy. First you have some time to look at Questions 1 to 4 now. You will see that there is an example which has been done for you. The conversation relating to this will be played first.
Tom: Well, here we are. There's certainly plenty to choose from.
Mary: I'm finding it hard to know where to start. Would you like to look at the answering machines?
Tom: Let's start there. I like this one.
Mary: We have a lot to buy, Tom. We can't afford to pay $129 for an answering machine. And we can't afford to pay $127.50 for the dual tape answering machine, either.
Tom: Alright. We'll buy a cheaper one then. There's this one for $89 or the smaller one for $59.95.
Mary: I like the square shape of the smaller one. It'll fit neatly on my desk.
Tom: And it's the cheapest. Okay. We'll buy that one.
Narrator: Tom and Mary choose the small, square answering machine costing $59.95, the cheapest available, so letter B has been circled. Now we shall begin. You should answer the questions as you listen because you will not hear the recording a second time. Now listen carefully and answer questions 1 to 4.
Tom: Well, here we are. There's certainly plenty to choose from.

Mary: I'm finding it hard to know where to start. Would you like to look at the answering machines?
Tom: Let's start there. I like this one.
Mary: We have a lot to buy, Tom. We can't afford to pay $129 for an answering machine. And we can't afford to pay $127.50 for the dual tape answering machine, either.
Tom: Alright. We'll buy a cheaper one then. There's this one for $89 or the smaller one for $59.95.
Mary: I like the square shape of the smaller one. It'll fit neatly onto my desk.
Tom: And it's the cheapest. Okay, we'll buy that one.
Mary: Good. Now, we need to buy a telephone for the office.
Tom: I'd like to get a portable phone. You know, one of those cordless ones.
Mary: Are you sure?
Tom: I think it's a good idea. We don't need another telephone answering machine, so we can look for a small one.
Mary: I really like the one with the hinge in the middle.
Tom: A folding telephone! Yes, that's a good idea. So we'll take that one. Are you ready to look at the other things we need?
Mary: Yes. Let me look at the list. We need a couple of radios.
Tom: I want one I can listen to while I'm walking.
Mary: I know. They're just over here. I don't think you should buy the really cheap one.
Tom: You mean this one? $17 is a very good price.
Mary: Ah, that's true, but I believe they give a very bad sound quality. And what if you want to use a cassette? It doesn't have any space for a cassette.
Tom: You're right. Hmm. Well, I really hate the ones where you have to put the small earphones into your ear.
Mary: Here's one with big earphones you put over your ears.

Tom: Ooh. It's expensive ...

Mary: It's only $20 more than the one with the little earphones. Take it!

Tom: Okay. What's next?

Mary: We have to choose a television.

Tom: We need one which is - ah - big enough to ...

Mary: But not too big. I don't want anything larger than 48 cm.

Tom: I really think 34 cm is too small for our room. That's only about thirteen and a half inches.

Mary: Okay. Let's take the size bigger than 34 cm.

Tom: What about another radio?

Mary: How would you feel about a clock radio instead of just a radio?

Tom: I don't want a clock radio. I'm very fond of my alarm clock! But I like this radio with the curved carry handle.

Mary: So do I. It's a good price, too. So, now we've chosen an answering machine, a cordless telephone, a radio for you to use when you go for a walk, another radio and a television.

Tom: Anything else?

Mary: No. Let's go and have a cup of coffee!

Narrator: Tom and Mary go for their cup of coffee. Listen to their conversation, and be ready to answer questions 5 to 10.

Now listen to the conversation between Tom and Mary, and answer questions 5 to 10. Write no more than three words for each answer.

Mary: Shopping's hard work!

Tom: I'm glad it's over.

Mary: Do you want to go home now?

Tom: Yes, I think I'll take the things we bought home.

Mary: Okay. I'll go to the office. I've got lots to do. I'll come back later, straight from the office.

Tom: Okay. I'd better hurry. My brother's waiting at the house to help carry the television in.

Mary: Good. I hope he'll still be there when I get home - I haven't seen your brother for ages. No, wait, I forgot to tell you. I'll be late home tonight. I've got a meeting at 5 o'clock.

Tom: When do you think it will end?

Mary: I'm not sure. Still, I should be home by eight. If I think I'll be later than 8 o'clock I'll call you.

Tom: Okay. It's nice now that your office is in City Square. You don't have to travel very far at all.

Mary: I certainly appreciate it! Taxi drivers always know where City Square is, too. By the way, are you going to watch People are Funny on TV tonight?

Tom: What did you say? What TV show? Oh, People are Funny? Of course I am. I'll tell you what happened when you get home. I need something to laugh at - I'm going to the new office at Newtown tomorrow, and I'm not looking forward to it.

Mary: I'd better go. Take care. I'll see you later. Bye bye.

Narrator: That is the end of Section 1. You now have some time to check your answers.

Now turn to Section 2.

Section 2. You are going to hear a student arranging to transfer between English classes. She is leaving a message on the language department's answering machine. The student's name is May Lee. First look at questions 11 to 17.

As you listen to the first part of the talk, answer questions 11 to 17.

May: Hello. This is May Lee speaking. This message is for Mrs Brooks, in student affairs. Mrs Brooks, I telephoned you last week and you told me to call back and put the details of my request to transfer on the answering machine. I hope you can hear me easily. I have the form here and I'll give you the information working from the top to the bottom. As you know, my family name is Lee, spelled L-E-E, and my first name is May. My student number is 002312, that's 002312. I'm in Mr Anderson's class - you know, he's the one who helps out with the football team.

The next part of the form asks for my address. I'll give it slowly. I live at Flat 5, 10 University Avenue - you probably know the building, it's just near the engineering school.

The telephone number is 818 6074, and I share it with a lot of other people so it's often engaged. I'll give it to you again, 818 6074. I think that's all I have to put on this part of the form. I know you were curious about my reason for requesting a transfer, so I'll explain that next.

Narrator: Now look at questions 18 to 22.

As May Lee continues her message, answer questions 18 to 22.

May: Now I'll tell you why I want a transfer between classes. Mrs Brooks, I really like my teacher and my classmates, but I find it very hard not to speak in my own language. I just begin to think in English when the class ends, and I'm surrounded by other people from my country so it's natural that we all speak in our mother tongue. I have been looking around for a class where there are very few other people from my country so I will be forced to use English.

The best class I can find is the evening class which begins at 6 pm. Most of the students in that class come from countries which speak Spanish, and I can't speak a word so I must use English. I have an Italian friend in the class, and she tells me there are two Hong Kong Chinese, six Spanish speakers and one Japanese student. She says most people speak English at the break, although sometimes the Spanish slip into their own language.

I checked the class list, and two students have dropped out of the evening class so there should be room for me. Could you please see if I can join the class? I'm not sure what the class number is, but the evening class I want is in Room 305 of the Trotter Building. The class I'm in now is next door to the Trotter building in Prince Tower, so it's very easy for me to find my way to the new class.

I'm not going home until late today, so could you please leave a message for me at my friend Margaret's house? Her number is 812 7543, and she has an answering machine.

I do hope you can transfer me, Mrs Brooks. If there is any more information you need please call me. Thank you very much.

Narrator: That is the end of Section 2. You will now

have some time to check your answers.
Now turn to Section 3.
Section 3. In this section you will hear a discussion between a tutor, Dr Lester, and two students, Greg and Alexandra, at the end of a talk about music. In the first part of the discussion they are talking about some of the students' favourite instruments, and favourite styles of music.
Complete the table showing the students' opinions. Choose your answers from the box. There are more words than spaces so you will not use them all. You may use any of the words more than once. First look at questions 23 to 27. Note the example that has been done for you.
Now listen to the first part and answer questions 23 to 27.
Dr Lester: I think it's time we looked at the results of our survey. Ah. What did you find out, Alexandra?
Alexandra: We're a group with very diverse tastes, Dr Lester.
Dr Lester: Hm. I'm not surprised. What were the favourite instruments?
Alexandra: Well, Greg loves drums. He told me he played drums when he was at primary school, and now he plays drums with his friends at weekends. They have a band.
Dr Lester: Hm. Good. Ah. What do you like to play, Alexandra?
Alexandra: My favourite is the guitar. However, I haven't played for years, so I keep hoping to start again. Will I go on with the others?
Dr Lester: Hm. Yes, please.
Alexandra: Katja is like Greg. She loves to listen to drums. She says she's not a player, just a listener. Rachel, as you know, is a violinist, so of course it's natural that she should favour the violin.
Dr Lester: Hm. So we have two people who love the sound of the drum and two who like strings - ah, the violin for Rachel and the guitar for Alex. What does Harry like?
Alexandra: Harry says the best instrument of them all is the piano. He claims it's more versatile than any other instrument. Emiko plays the piano, but her favourite instrument is the flute.
Dr Lester: The flute?
Alexandra: Yes. Emiko plays the flute too, of course.
Dr Lester: Hm. Thank you, Alexandra. Ah, Greg, will you tell us the students' favourite style of music?
Greg: We're really very conservative. My favourite is classical music, and that's Alexandra's choice too. Katja claims to like rock.
Dr Lester: So that's a vote from Greg, Alexandra and Katja. Doesn't Rachel prefer classical music?
Greg: Rachel made a choice which surprised me. She plays the violin, so I expected classical or opera, but Rachel says that she prefers country music.
Dr Lester: Hm. How interesting! What's Harry's choice?
Greg: Harry likes to listen to opera, and loves to go to see a performance. He says opera has everything, colour and spectacle and theatre and great music.
Dr Lester: And Emiko?
Greg: Emiko says jazz is her favourite music. She goes to listen to jazz every Friday evening. She also likes

opera, heavy metal, classical ... but jazz is the best.
Dr Lester: Thank you, Greg. I wanted to see what you all liked so I could understand your musical tastes more, and I want to move from this to a discussion of the physiological effects of music.
Narrator: In the second part of the discussion Dr Lester will talk about the way music affects our bodies. Look at questions 28 to 31 first. As you listen to the discussion, complete the sentences.
Dr Lester: For the purposes of this discussion, I'm going to divide music roughly into two types: music which stimulates us and music which calms us. It seems that music which stimulates us gives rise to actual changes in our bodies. We listen to exciting music and our hearts beat faster, our blood pressure rises, and our blood flows more quickly. In short, we're stimulated. Soothing music, however, has the opposite effect. We relax, and let the world go by. Our heart beats more gently, our blood pressure drops, and we feel calm. Um Alexandra, can you think of things which help us to relax?
Alexandra: Um. Gentle rhythms?
Dr Lester: Yes, in part. The melodies which help us to relax are smooth flowing and often have repeated rhythms. These rhythms are constant and dynamic, a little like the crash of the sea on the beach. Their very predictability is sedating, relaxing. By contrast very loud, discordant music with unpredictable rhythms and structures excites and stimulates us. These two generalisations about the differences between music which stimulates and music which soothes are true as far as they go, but they are far from conclusive. We still have a lot of research to do to find out what, ah, for instance, people of different cultures hear and feel when they listen to music. This department is taking part in a continuing study on the influence of culture on musical perception, and we'll talk about that more next week.
Narrator: That is the end of Section 3. You will now have some time to check your answers.
This side of the tape is now complete. Practice Listening Test 2 continues on side B. Please turn the tape over.
Tape 1 Side B Practice Listening Test 2 continues. Now turn to Section 4.
Section 4. You will hear an extract from a talk about preventative medicine - specifically, how students can look after their own health. Listen to what the speaker says, and answer questions 32 to 40. First you have some time to look at the questions. Now listen carefully and answer questions 32 to 36.
Parker: Good morning. I'm Dr Pat Parker, and I'm here to talk to you about preventative medicine in its widest and most personal aspects. In other words, I'm here to tell you how the patient should wrest control of their health away from the practitioners of medicine and take charge of their own medical destiny. I want to talk about staying out of the hands of the doctor.
When the patient takes responsibilty for her or his own health - and let's decide the patient is male for now - men are in fact more at risk than women

anyway - when the patient takes over his own health regime he must decide what he wants to do. The first thing, of course, is to give up the demon nicotine. Smoking is the worst threat to health, and it's self-inflicted damage. I have colleagues who are reluctant to treat smokers. If you want to stay well, stay off tobacco and smoking in all its manifestations. Our department has recently completed a survey of men's health. We looked at men in different age groups and occupations, and we came up with a disturbing insight. Young men, particularly working class men, are at considerable risk of premature death because of their life style. As a group, they have high risk factors: they drink too much alcohol, they smoke more heavily than any other group, their diet is frequently heavy in saturated fats, and they don't get enough exercise.

We then did a smaller survey in which we looked at environmental factors which affect health. I had privately expected to find air or water pollution to be the biggest hazards, and they must not be ignored. However, the effects of the sun emerged as a threat which people simply do not take sufficiently seriously. Please remember that too much sunlight can cause permanent damage.

Given this information, and the self-destructive things which people, particularly young men, are doing to themselves, one could be excused for feeling very depressed. However, I believe that a well-funded education campaign will help us improve public health standards and will be particularly valuable for young men. I'm an optimist. I see things improving, but only if we work very hard. In the second part of the talk I want to consider different things that you as students can do to improve your fitness.

Narrator: Now answer questions 37 to 40.

Parker: So now I'd like to issue a qualification to everything I say. People will still get sick, and they will still need doctors. This advice is just to reduce the incidence of sickness - it would be great if disease were preventable, but it's not. However, we have power. In the late 80's the Surgeon-General of the United States said that 53 percent of our illnesses could be avoided by healthy lifestyle choices. I now want to discuss these choices with you.

You should try to make keeping fit fun! It's very hard to go out and do exercises by yourself, so it's wise to find a sport that you like and play it with other people. If you swim, you can consider scuba diving or snorkelling. If you jog, try to find a friend to go with. If you walk, choose pretty places to walk or have a reason for walking. Your exercise regime should be a pleasure, not a penance.

The university is an excellent place to find other people who share sporting interests with you, and there are many sports teams you can join. This, unfortunately, raises the issue of sports injuries, and different sports have characteristic injuries. As well as accidental injuries, we find repetitive strain injuries occurring in sports where the same motion is frequently performed, like rowing and squash. The parallel in working life is repetitive strain injury which may be suffered by typists or other people who perform the same action hour after hour, day after day.

In this context, therefore, the most important thing to remember before any sport is to warm up adequately. Do stretching exercises, and aim at all times to increase your flexibility. Be gentle with yourself, and allow time to prepare for the game you have chosen to play. Don't be fooled by the term "warm up", by the way. It's every bit as important to do your warm up exercises on a hot day as on a cool one.

I think one of the most sensible and exciting developments in the reduction of injury is the recognition that all sports can borrow from each other. Many sports programmes are now encouraging players to use cross training techniques, that is, to borrow training techniques from other sports. Boxers have been using cross training for years: building up stamina by doing road work and weight training, while honing their skills and reflexes. Other sports which require a high level of eye-hand coordination are following this trend, so you see table tennis players running and jogging to improve their performance, and footballers doing flexibility exercises which can help them control the ball better. All of these results are good, but the general sense of well-being is best, and is accessible to us all, from trained athletes to people who will never run a 100 metres in less than 15 seconds. Good health is not only for those who will achieve athletic greatness!

Narrator: That is the end of Section 4. Now you have some time to check your answers.

That is the end of Listening Practice 2.

Answer Key: Academic Practice Listening Test 3

Section 1	Section 2	Section 3	Section 4
Questions 1-8	Questions 9-19	Questions 20-30	Questions 31-38

Section 1 — Questions 1-8

1. ✓
2. ✓
3. ✓
4. 7.00-9.00 am
5. 6.00-8.00 pm
6. E
7. F
8. C

Section 2 — Questions 9-19

9. (The) Blue Mountains
10. Monday / Mon. / June 10(th) / 10/6
11. (the) front gate
12. 8 am
13. (the) side gate
14. 6 pm
15. (your / their) (own) lunch
16. strong shoes
17. 11 am
18. First Aid kit
19. 3B

Section 3 — Questions 20-30

20. 8 am-8 pm / 8-8
21. 9 am-9 pm / 9-9
22. 24 hours
23. E (up to) 6
24. A 2
25. E 3
26. B and D
27. E and F
28. 8 to 10 (am)
29. 200 / two hundred
30. a nurse / nursing

Section 4 — Questions 31-38

31. died (in 1900)
32. co-educational
33. ten / 10
34. teacher / university teacher
35. tolerance / debate / discussion
36. A
37. C
38. D

Tapescript: Practice Listening Test 3

Cassette 1 Side B

Narrator: Prepare for IELTS Practice Listening Tests.Practice Listening Test 3. Turn to Section 1 of Practice Listening Test 3.

Section 1. You have just arrived at the student hostel where you will live during the term. The manager is explaining the rules, and another student is asking questions. Listen to the conversation and complete the form. First you have some time to look at Questions 1 to 5 on the Student Hostel Charges for meals form now. You will see that there is an example which has been done for you. The conversation relating to this will be played first.

Student: Excuse me. I want to ask you about the charges for meals. Are they the same as they were last year?

Manager: No, I'm afraid they're not. We've managed to keep most of them the same, but we've had to increase the charge for breakfast.

Student: How much is it now?

Manager: It's $2.50. It used to be $2.00.

Student: I see. What about lunch?

Manager: It's unchanged - still $3.00.

Narrator: Breakfast costs $2.50, so the change has been written in. Lunch still costs $3.00, so the information has been ticked. Now we shall begin. You should answer the questions as you listen because you will not hear the recording a second time.

Now listen carefully and answer questions 1 to 5.

Student: Excuse me. I want to ask you about the charges for meals. Are they the same as they were last year?

Manager: No, I'm afraid they're not. We've managed to keep most of them the same, but we've had to increase the charge for breakfast.

Student: How much is it now?

Manager: It's $2.50. It used to be $2.00.

Student: I see. What about lunch?

Manager: It's unchanged - still $3.00.

Student: Does dinner still cost $3.00?

Manager: Yes, it does. We've managed to keep the prices down this year. But the best deal is the three meal plan for $48.00 per week. We give you vouchers to present when you come into the cafeteria, and you get twenty one meals for your $48. That works out to a little more than $2 a meal. The two meal plan is also at last year's rates of $36.00 per week. We give you vouchers for that, too.

Student: My sister was in this hostel before me. I'm sure the hours for breakfast used to be longer.

Manager: Yes, they were. They used to be 7 to 9.30, but to keep our expenses down we made them 7 to 9.

Student: Lunch is the way it was, though. Hold on! Dinner 6 to 7.30? Isn't that a change?

Manager: Yes, it is, and in fact the form is wrong. It used to be 5.30 to 7.30, but now it's 6 to 8 pm.

Student: 6 to 8 pm. That's good.

Manager: So which plan would you like?

Student: I'd like to think about it, please. I need to check my lecture schedule.

Narrator: Now look at questions 6 to 8. Listen to the conversation between the student and the manager and match the places in questions 6 to 8 to the appropriate letters A to F on the map.

Student: Can you tell me how to get to my room, please?

Manager: Of course. You're in the new wing, which is very freshly painted and pleasant. But I'm afraid you're going to have to go to a couple of other offices before you can have the key. You're in the Admissions Office now. Leave this office and turn right and go to the end of the hall. The last office is the fees office, where you can pay the balance of your room deposit. They'll give you a receipt.

Student: Okay.

Manager: After you've been to the fees office come back past Admissions. You'll see a very large room at the north western corner of the building. You can't miss it. That's the student lounge, and if you go in there you can meet some of the other students and see who'll have a room near you.

Student: That's good. Can I get a cup of coffee there?

Manager: Yes, there's a vending machine in the corner. Then go to the Key Room, which is opposite the lift and next to the library, show them your receipt, and you can pick up your key there.

Student: My luggage was sent on ahead. Do you know where I should collect it?

Manager: The box room is next to the women's toilet. You'll have to get the key from the key room.

Student: Thank you.

Narrator: That is the end of Section 1. You will now have some time to check your answers.

Now turn to Section 2.

Section 2. You are going to hear a teacher helping high school students visiting from an overseas school to fill in a school excursion permission note. First look at questions 9 to 16.

Listen while a teacher tells you how to complete the school excursion permission note. Write no more than three words or numbers for each answer.

Mrs Brown: Good morning students. My name is Mrs Brown, and I'm in charge of the school excursion next week. Please take out your School Excursion Permission Note so you can fill it in. For insurance purposes, this note must be signed by your guardian or the group leader. First of all, fill in the name of your class. Everyone here is in 3A, aren't they? So write 3A where it says "class". We're going to the Blue Mountains, which is great, so this is the school excursion to the Blue Mountains. The day we leave is Monday that's Monday June 10. We are travelling by bus all the way, so we don't have to worry about changing trains or anything like that. The bus will leave from the front gate at 8 am. I know we usually use the side gate, but because of the roadworks we will be using the front gate when we leave. However, when we return the roadwork will be complete so we'll use the side gate. We expect to be back at 6 pm.

It's going to be a lovely day. Your teachers will give you tasks to do when we arrive. We'll provide fruit and fruit juice on the bus, but you must bring your own lunch.

While we're on the excursion we'll be moving around a lot in some fairly rough country. Be very careful to wear strong shoes. It's very important that you look after your feet very well. Now does anyone have any questions they want to ask?

Narrator: Now look at questions 17 to 19.

As the talk continues, answer questions 17 to 19. Write no more than three words or numbers for each answer.

Mrs Brown: No questions? Okay. I'd just like to fill in a few more details. The bus should arrive in the Blue Mountains at 11 am. We'll have time to do the first of our tasks before lunch. The bus is not a new one, but it does carry one piece of special equipment - a first aid kit. I certainly hope we won't have to use it, but it's nice to know it's there in case we have a medical emergency.

The other class on this excursion is 3B, so I know it'll be a good day. The last time 3A and 3B went out together was a thoroughly successful excursion.

Narrator: That is the end of Section 2. You will now have some time to check your answers.

Now turn to Section 3.

Section 3. In this section you will hear a conversation between Mrs Lam, a member of the staff in a large hospital, and Andrew, who is a student in the nursing school. Mrs Lam is explaining the rules about visiting hours in the hospital. Look at questions 20 to 25.

Listen to the first part of the conversation and answer questions 20 to 22. Complete the table showing when visitors may go to the different parts of the hospital.

Mrs Lam: Hello, Andrew. I believe you want to know about visiting hours?

Andrew: Yes, I do Mrs Lam. I have to fill this form out, and I'd like to have some idea why the different parts of the hospital have different times for visiting.

Mrs Lam: I see. Well, let's start with an obvious one. Intensive Care. People in intensive care are very sick indeed, and for that reason we say that visitors can come between 6 am and midnight.

Andrew: I can understand that.

Mrs Lam: At the other end of the scale, our maternity patients are usually quite well, but we restrict their visiting hours from 8 am to 8 pm. We find they get very tired if we permit visitors all the time.

Andrew: I see. What about the surgical wards?

Mrs Lam: The doctors prefer to do their rounds early in surgical, so visiting hours are 9 am to 9 pm. Surgical patients are often on very heavy painkillers, and they aren't really very good company for their visitors!

Andrew: But surely the visitors come to cheer up the patient, not the other way round?

Mrs Lam: Of course. And often the visitors are able to help the patient a lot. That's why we allow visitors all day, the full 24 hours, in the emergency ward. They help comfort the patient while they're waiting to be diagnosed.

Narrator: In the second part of the discussion Andrew will ask Mrs Lam about the people who are allowed to visit patients. Look at questions 23 to 25 first. Complete the table showing who is allowed to visit, and the number of visitors permitted. Use the letter **A** to show that **Adults** may visit, **E** to show that **Everyone** may visit and **I** to show that only **Immediate** family may visit.

Mrs Lam: Of course, it's not just everyone who can visit a sick patient. People in intensive care can only be visited by their immediate family. What's more, we only allow two people in at any time. We let children of the immediate family in to visit people in intensive care, but we don't like to do it. It's very hard on the children, and it may distress the patient. However, if the patient asks for the child, and the family agrees, that's okay.

Andrew: What about children in maternity?

Mrs Lam: Of course we let them in! They're very pleased to see their mothers. The rule in maternity is everyone may visit, up to six people at a time. The maternity ward is quite sociable, after all.

Andrew: The surgical ward must be different.

Mrs Lam: It is indeed. We don't allow children in

the surgical ward because of the danger of infection, and as you know we restrict the hours. There are a lot of procedures which must be carried out on surgical patients, and we only let two visitors come in at a time.

Andrew: And in Emergency, people are allowed to visit all the time?

Mrs Lam: Oh yes. We rely on patients' relatives to be there for them, and we permit everyone to visit the emergency department at all hours. However, we restrict it to three visitors for each patient. Otherwise the room just gets totally crowded.

Narrator: Now listen to Mrs Lam explaining where Andrew will spend the first week of his training. Circle two letters. An example has been done for you. Look at questions 26 and 27.

Circle two letters in each answer.

Mrs Lam: Now I have your schedule for the next week's observation sessions. Are you ready?

Andrew: Yes. Where do I start?

Mrs Lam: On Monday you'll be in male surgical in the morning, and in female surgical in the afternoon. You'll be following Dr Shay on her rounds.

Andrew: Thank you. And on Tuesday?

Mrs Lam: On Tuesday you will be with Dr Thomas in the morning and Dr Robertson in the afternoon. No, that can't be right … you're with Dr Thomas in the afternoon and Dr Robertson in the morning.

Andrew: Do I ever get to see Dr Kim ?

Mrs Lam: Yes, you'll be with Dr Kim on Thursday and Friday. She'll take you through the children's ward and through our new teenage ward for 12 to 15 year olds.

Andrew: Great! I've read a lot about that new ward. Will I see the school room?

Mrs Lam: Maybe another time.

Narrator: Now look at questions 28 to 30.

Now answer questions 28 to 30. Write no more than three words or numbers for each answer.

Andrew: And what will I do on Wednesday?

Mrs Lam: On Wednesday you'll join the other students for lectures. You'll be in the Redmore Lecture Room between 8 and 10 am and later between 2 and 3 pm.

Andrew: Thank you. Do you know how big my class is?

Mrs Lam: The intake this term is two hundred first year students. I'm pleased to say about one third are men, which is good. Nursing used to be an almost entirely female occupation.

Andrew: I know. My father trained as a nurse, and he was considered very unusual.

Mrs Lam: Is he still working as a nurse?

Andrew: Yes. He's working in a hospital in the country. I guess I just wanted to follow his example.

Narrator: That is the end of Section 3. You will now have some time to check your answers.

Now turn to Section 4.

Section 4. You will hear an extract from an introductory talk given to a group of students who have just entered a university residential college. The speaker is the principal of the college.

Listen to what the speaker says, and answer questions 31 to 38. First you have some time to look at questions 31 to 35.

Now listen carefully and answer questions 31 to 35.

Principal: Good morning, and welcome to Scholastic House. I am delighted to see you here. It is my duty to explain to you some of the history of our college and some of the traditions which I hope you will uphold. The idea for Scholastic House was expounded by Samuel Wells in 1898. Wells was a visionary, whose ideas were well ahead of his time. He wanted a college which would encourage friendship between people of different races and nationalities. Wells died in 1900 before he could see the college in action. Scholastic House finally began operating in 1903 with ten students. Those students came from Asia, Europe, and the Americas. At that time Scholastic House accepted only male students, although it has been co-educational since 1963. Nine of these foundation students went on to lead illustrious lives; the only exception died tragically on his way home from Scholastic House to Sarawak. He had only recently graduated with an honours degree in Law, and he was robbed of a brilliant future.

The other nine students, as I said, led very fulfilling lives. Three became political leaders, three became doctors. Perhaps the most famous graduate became a university teacher and was responsible for the introduction of modern teaching training methods in his country. Two of the original group became senior engineers and went on to deeply influence the way the water systems of their country were exploited. The college ran into hard times during the period of the Great War, 1914 to 1918, when the charter of the college was interpreted to mean that neither students nor staff could take part in the war effort. Many people felt that this indicated a lack of national spirit, and the walls of the college were frequently marked with graffiti. Meantime, outside the college, tens of thousands of young men went away to fight in Europe, never to return.

The college was building a reputation for learning and for tolerance of opposing views. Scholastic House debate and discussion nights were opened to the public in 1927, and have been available to anyone who wishes to attend ever since. It is a proud tradition of the college that any view may be expressed provided that it can be defended intellectually. Over the years topics which were controversial at the time have been discussed and debated.

Narrator: Now look at questions 36 to 38.

Principal: As I said, the college has a proud history of publicly examining controversial issues. Why should we do this? The publicity we receive is often sensational, and there is no joy in encouraging argument for its own sake; in fact that sort of discussion just increases tension. The only legitimate reason for our behaviour is that it casts light upon the topic in question and informs the debate.

And controversial topics are the ones which most need informed attention. As the world forges ahead we often find our scientists have outstripped our philosophers. We frequently develop scientific marvels without realising their full implications. Nowhere is this more obvious than in medicine. We are now able to keep people alive far longer than before, but this medical ability must be measured in relation to the quality of those lives.

I urge you to spend your time at Scholastic House wisely. You are the heirs of an excellent academic tradition of which we can all be justly proud.

It is your responsibility to continue this tradition of querying where our world is going. Progress is not always upwards.

I wish you every joy in your time here, and I hope that I will hear much well informed debate from you.

Narrator: That is the end of Section 4. Now you have some time to check your answers.

That is the end of Listening Practice Test 3.

This tape is now complete.

Practice Listening Test 4 starts on Cassette 2 Side A.

Academic Practice Listening Test 4

Answer Key: Academic Practice Listening Test 4

Section 1 Questions 1-8	Section 2 Questions 9-18	Section 3 Questions 19-29	Section 4 Questions 30-39
1. C	9. ✓	19. water wheel	30. hunger
2. T	10. 11 (pm)	20. gears	31. noise
3. CT	11. 11.30 (pm)	21. spray tube	32. study
4. CST	12. ✓	22. holes	33. tense
5. T	13. ✓	23. base	34. tired
6. T	14. Thurs / Thursday	24. C	35. 45 degrees
7. S	15. Smith Street	25. A	36. relaxed
8. C	16. laying (telephone) cable(s)	26. A	37. chew
	17. (the) college grounds	27. A	38. exercise
	18. side door	28. B	39. smoky
		29. D	

Tapescript: Practice Listening Test 4

Cassette 2 Side A
Narrator: Prepare for IELTS Practice Listening tests. This is tape 2

Prepare for IELTS Practice Listening Tests. Practice Listening Test 4.

Turn to Section 1 of Practice Listening Test 4.

Section 1. Listen to the conversation between two students, John and Carol. They have a list of the names of authors whose books have been given to the library. They have to classify the authors as writers of cookery, sports or travel. First you have some time to look at Questions 1 to 8 on the table now.

You will see that there is an example which has been done for you. The conversation relating to this will be played first.

John: This is a great collection of books, isn't it?
Carol: Very impressive. Who gave them to us?
John: Apparently the donor was a book reviewer. There are a lot of books about sport. Here's one. *My life in cricket.*

Carol: That's certainly sports. Who's the author?
John: Peter Adams.
Carol: He also wrote *Journeys through Spain.*
John: Did he?
Narrator: Peter Adams writes on both sports and travel, so S T is written against his name.

Now we shall begin. You should answer the questions as you listen because you will not hear the recording a second time. Now listen carefully and answer questions 1 to 8.

John: This is a great collection of books, isn't it?
Carol: Very impressive. Who gave them to us?
John: Apparently the donor was a book reviewer. There are a lot of books about sport. Here's one. *My life in cricket.*
Carol: That's certainly sports. Who's the author?
John: Peter Adams.
Carol: He also wrote *Journeys through Spain.*
John: Did he?
Carol: Next one is Stephen Bau.
John: He wrote *Summer Barbecues, Cooking for Singles, Dinners by Candlelight ...*
Carol: Anything else?

John: No. Do you have anything by Pam Campbell?

Carol: *Wanderings in Greece, My life in Russia, Travels in the Amazon,* and *Pam Campbell's guide to a successful trip.*

John: Sounds like she got around! My next one is C. Kezik.

Carol: He has a list of books about football. *The World Cup, Heroes of the World Cup, Playing with the round ball, Soccer for everyone ...*

John: That's enough! He was a one-topic writer. Ari Hussein, however, wrote about cooking and travel! His series of cook books is called *Living and cooking in Spain, Living and cooking in China, Living and cooking in Brazil.* He's been everywhere.

Carol: I've got a specialist here. Sally Innes on tennis. Here are some of her titles: *Improve your serve, Tennis for everyone, Tennis forever!*

John: Meg Jorgensen has three books, one in each category: *Cooking for health, Sport is good for you!* and *Travelling in Australia.*

Carol: A varied talent. Who's next?

John: Bruno Murray. He wrote children's books - a whole series called *A child's guide to ...* and then the name of the city.

Carol: Oh. You mean like *A child's guide to London*?

John: Yes, that's right. He seems to have stayed in Europe. Ruby Lee, however, has just one book. It's called *The emerald isle* and it's all about Ireland. Apparently she went around Ireland on foot.

Carol: Jim Wells wouldn't like that! His books are all about motor racing. Hmm. Nice photos of old racing cars. Don't you love the goggles on the driver?

John: They do look strange, don't they? I think we're nearly finished. What did Helen Yeung write?

Carol: *Summer menus: food for thought.* She also did a book of Chinese recipes - Cantonese, I think.

John: Okay. That's dealt with the first box. Let's stop for a minute.

Narrator: That is the end of Section 1. You now have some time to check your answers.

Now turn to Section 2.

Section 2. You are going to hear a talk by a student adviser who is inviting new students to a welcoming party. Look at the invitation. Tick if the information is correct or write in the changes. First look at questions 9 to 14.

As you listen to the first part of the talk, answer questions 9 to 14.

Student Adviser: Hello. My name is Dave Burns, and I'm here to tell you about the welcoming party we are having for new students. Unfortunately the information on your invitation is inaccurate. We didn't have enough time to print new invitations, so I'll have to ask you to make changes.

To start with, this isn't a welcoming lunch: it's a dance party. However, the next line is true. The party will be held at Blackwell House. Is everybody comfortable with that? The next line tells you when the party will be: Friday June 15th at 8 pm, but I have good news: the party will end at 11 pm. As a result of this later end to the party the bus will go later, too, so it should read "Free transport to the student

hostel is available leaving Blackwell House at 11.30". And of course other students may attend, and all students must have their student ID card with them. I hope you can come to the welcoming party. It's a really good way to get to know other students and to learn what it's like to live in this city and to study here. Just one final change: please let us know by Thursday if you can come.

Narrator: Now listen while Dave Burns gives instructions for students who are going to travel by car to the party. First look at questions 15 to 18. Write no more than three words for each answer.

Student Adviser: Some of you may prefer to travel by car, but I have to warn you about some changes to the roads. You will find there is a lot of new road work on Smith Street. The work will not finish for a long time so we can be sure that Smith Street will be a problem.

If you are coming from the city you will be able to travel easily until you get to Blackwell Street, just near the college. As you know Blackwell Street is very long. You should avoid the corner of Blackwell Street and Jones Avenue, because they are laying telephone cable. However, you can take a detour and avoid Blackwell Street altogether. The best thing to do is to pass the round-about and take the first road on your left which is Brown Crescent. Brown Crescent will lead you into the college grounds, so that's easy. I hope everyone has a great time. Bring your friends, and we'll see you on Friday. Oh, one final reminder: it's best to use the side door. The front door may be locked at 7.00, so come to the side. See you on Friday.

Narrator: That is the end of Section 2. You will now have some time to check your answers.

Now turn to Section 3.

Section 3. In this section you will hear a discussion between two students who have to describe a lawn sprinkler for part of their general science course. (A lawn sprinkler is a machine designed to water gardens and lawns). In the first part of the discussion the students are talking about the different parts of the sprinkler. First look at questions 19 to 23. Note the example that has been done for you.

Now listen to the conversation and label the parts of the sprinkler on the diagram. Choose from the box. There are more words in the box than you will need.

Linda: Hello, Scott! I believe you're going to be my partner for this practical session. Have you got the model set up?

Scott: Yes. Uh. It's right here. The instructions say we have to describe it first, and label the diagram. I've started from where the water enters the machine. Um. The water enters through a hose pipe and then it turns a water wheel. You can see where the wheel is marked by an arrow pointing upwards. It's called a water wheel because it's designed so the water will catch against the wheel. This action spins a series of gears ...

Linda: How are you going to describe the gears?

Scott: There are two worm gears, one vertical and one horizontal. The horizontal worm gear drives a circular gear. That gear is connected to a crank which changes the motion. The crank is already labelled.

Do you see the two white arrows?

Linda: I see. Okay, the water has passed across the water wheel. Then what?

Scott: Okay. Umm. Then you could say the water passes through the spray tube.

Linda: Yes, I see.

Scott: And the water is then spread over the lawn through holes at the top of the spray tube.

Linda: How are you going to describe the base?

Scott: How about this: "The sprinkler stands on a base consisting of two metal tubes which join at a hinge at one end and continue into a plastic moulding at the other."

Linda: That's certainly starting at the bottom. Do you want to mention that there's no water in the base?

Scott: I don't think that's necessary. If you look at the diagram it's easy to see that the only metal tube to contain water is the spray tube. You can actually see the water coming out of it.

Narrator: Now listen while Linda and Scott's instructor, Mark Stewart, talks to them. Answer questions 24 to 29.

Mark: Hello Scott, Linda. I'm glad I caught you before class. Did you know about the change in the examination schedule?

Scott: Change?

Mark: Yes. The last day of examinations for your group will be December 2nd instead of November 29th.

Scott: Is that definite? We were told they'd be on November 26, and then there was a rumour they'd be on December the 1st.

Mark: The schedule's gone to the printer. There can be no changes. It's definitely December 2nd.

Scott: That's a relief. I'm going to the US on December the 4th.

Mark: Are you one of the exchange students?

Scott: Yeah. Yeah. I'm really looking forward to studying there. Do you know if their general science courses are anything like ours?

Linda: It's not very likely.

Mark: Actually, all basic general science courses are fairly similar. You'll find you're behind in some things and ahead in others. I wouldn't worry too much about the course. You've been doing well on this one. Linda, have you finished your assignment yet?

Linda: I'm nearly there. I should be able to give it to you on Monday.

Mark: That's good. I can't let you have another extension.

Linda: I was really grateful for the extra time you gave me. That was a really big assignment.

Mark: Well, I'll expect it next week. Now, would you like to hear the details of the timetable?

Scott: Oh. Yes, please.

Mark: I've just finished putting it on the noticeboard downstairs. Basically, you'll have four examinations. General mechanics is in the morning of December 1st, physics and maths are on the afternoon of the same day. Communications and English are on the morning of December 2nd, and Earth Sciences in the afternoon.

Linda: All over in two days!

Mark: Yes. I'll miss teaching this class. You're all good at expressing your views, which makes for an interesting class. Some of the other first year classes won't talk, and they're rather boring to teach.

Narrator: That is the end of Section 3. You will now have some time to check your answers.

Now turn to Section 4.

Section 4. You will hear an extract from a talk about student health, and specifically about ways to avoid headaches. Listen to what the speaker says, and complete the summary. First look at questions 30 to 39. As you listen to the talk, answer questions 30 to 39. Complete the summary. Use words from the box. There are more words in the box than you need. Some words may be used more than once.

Broadcaster: Hello. Welcome to the student orientation program. Today's session is on health issues, and this talk is about headaches, and how to avoid them. It may surprise you to hear that headaches are often caused by hunger! In fact one study suggested that 70% of headaches are related to hunger, which makes it the principal cause. The advice is simple: eat three meals a day and try to keep to a fairly regular schedule of meals. People associate noise with headaches, and for most of us excessive noise creates the conditions for a headache. Very loud noise is unpleasant, and people usually remove themselves from it. Having said that, younger people tend to tolerate noise better than their elders, so I may be leaving noisy places far earlier than you. Just remember that exposure to too much noise may predispose you to a headache. Of course, we all associate headaches with studying! In fact the headache probably doesn't come from the studying so much as from being tense. When we study hard, we often hunch over our work. Try raising your shoulders and tensing them - now relax. Can you feel how much more comfortable a relaxed stance is? Another thing - it's very important to check that you are working in a good light. It will not actually hurt your eyes to work in a bad light, but it will make you tired very quickly and is very likely to give you a headache. What's more, if you have the book flat on a desk in front of you it will be harder to read, and you will have to hold your head at an odd angle. It is wise to have a bookrest which raises the material you are reading 45 degrees to the desk. This will help reduce your chance of a headache. Try to relax before bed so that you will be relaxed when you try to sleep - a soak in a hot bath may be helpful. It's also important to really sleep when you go to bed: a good mattress is a wise investment for people who want to avoid headaches.

This talk seems to keep coming back to tension. Tension may cause you to chew too forcefully, clench your jaw, or grind your teeth, and this in turn may lead to headaches. It is very easy to say that you shouldn't grind your teeth, and very hard to stop, particularly if you grind your teeth in your sleep. Try to avoid situations which will make you tense, particularly just before bed. If you do compulsively grind your teeth in your sleep, ask your dentist about a soft mouthguard.

In general, try to eat regular meals and avoid tense situations. Be sure you get plenty of exercise. Hopefully your headaches will be greatly reduced. One other thing I should point out - avoid smoky rooms and cars. Such places certainly encourage headaches, and the smoke may be doing you quite serious long-term damage.

Narrator: That is the end of Section 4. Now you have some time to check your answers.

That is the end of Test 4. Test 5 is on Cassette 2 Side B.

Academic Practice Listening Test 5

Answer Key: Academic Practice Listening Test 5

Section 1 Questions 1-7	Section 2 Questions 10-20	Section 3 Questions 21-31	Section 4 Questions 32-40
1. A	8. 3	21. 1987	32. A
2. B	9. 5	22. Turkey	33. C
3. D	10. 8.25 (AM)	23. English for farming	34. B
4. A	11. coach	24. 16 weeks / 4 months	35. D
5. D	12. 2	25. 14 (students)	36. B
6. C	13. Friday	26. former / previous / old students	37. A
7. A	14. (sailing) boat	27. advanced (students)	38. Social life
	15. (Greek) music	28. all (students)	39. Hide (extra) fees
	16. B; D	28. advanced (students)	40. The government
	17. A; B	30. all (students)	
	18. B; D	31. beginners	
	19. Greek tour		
	20. AA3 *(not aa3)*		

Tapescript: Practice Listening Test 5

Cassette 2 Side B
Narrator: Prepare for IELTS Practice Listening tests. Practice Listening Test 5. Turn to Section 1 of Practice Listening Test 5.

Section 1. Megan and Ken are deciding how they will spend the evening. Look at section 1 of your listening test. You have some time to look at Questions 1 to 7 now. You will see that there is an example which has been done for you. The conversation relating to this will be played first.

Telephone rings
Megan: Hello. Megan speaking.
Ken: Hello Megan.
Megan: Hello Ken. I'm glad you called. Thomas asked me to give you his telephone number.
Ken: Is that his office number or his home number?
Megan: I can give you both. His new home number is 9452 3456. Would you like his office number?
Ken: I think I have it. Does 9731 4322 sound right?
Megan: That's it. But the home number is 9452 3456. He moved in last week.
Ken: Good. I've got that. Now, what would you like to do?

Narrator: Thomas's home telephone number is 9452 3456 so letter C has been circled. Now we shall begin. You should answer the questions as you listen because you will not hear the questions a second time. First, you have another chance to look at questions 1 to 7. Now listen carefully and answer questions 1 to 7.

Telephone rings
Megan: Hello. Megan speaking.
Ken: Hello Megan.
Megan: Hello Ken. I'm glad you called. Thomas asked me to give you his telephone number.
Ken: Is that his office number or his home number?
Megan: I can give you both. His new home number is 9452 3456. Would you like his office number?
Ken: I think I have it. Does 9731 4322 sound right?
Megan: That's it. But the home number is 9452 3456. He moved in last week.
Ken: Good. I've got that. Now, what would you like to do?

Narrator: Thomas's home telephone number is 9452 3456 so letter C has been circled. Now we shall begin. You should answer the recording as you listen because you will not hear the questions a second time. First, you have another chance to look at questions 1 to 7. Now listen carefully and answer questions 1 to 7.

Telephone rings

Megan: Hello. Megan speaking.

Ken: Hello Megan.

Megan: Hello Ken. I'm glad you called. Thomas asked me to give you his telephone number.

Ken: Is that his office number or his home number?

Megan: I can give you both. His new home number is 9452 3456. Would you like his office number?

Ken: I think I have it. Does 9731 4322 sound right?

Megan: That's it. But the home number is 9452 3456. He moved in last week.

Ken: Good. I've got that. Now, what would you like to do?

Megan: Well, I'd like to go dancing, but Jane's hurt her ankle so she'd rather not.

Ken: That's a pity. I guess it means she doesn't want to play tennis, either.

Megan: That's right. She says it's okay to go bowling if we don't expect her to do well.

Ken: Okay, let's do it! I guess we can go dancing another time.

Megan: Well, I booked us some time at the bowling alley of Entertainment City. Do you know it?

Ken: Is it on Smith Street, down near the university?

Megan: That's right. It's on the corner of Smith Street and Bridge Road.

Ken: What time did you book for?

Megan: The first booking I could get was 8 o'clock.

Ken: Okay. It's 7 now. What do you want to do first?

Megan: Well, I think we should leave now. We can meet at the bowling alley.

Ken: I can't be that quick. I have to call Thomas, to start with, and I need to get changed.

Megan: Okay. I think I'll leave in ten minutes and meet you in there.

Ken: That makes sense. I'll take my car, so I'll be quite quick. I'll be out of here in half an hour.

Megan: Okay. You're so lucky to have a car! You can get around so easily.

Ken: Well, yes and no. I often spend ages driving around trying to find a park. The traffic can be very bad.

Megan: Well, that won't be a problem for me, because I'll take the bus. It goes right past my door, and I'll have plenty of time.

Ken: Sounds good. Who else is coming?

Megan: I think nearly everyone from the afternoon class will be there.

Ken: Which class? The big maths class, or the afternoon tutorial?

Megan: The maths class. What's more, we get a concession for large numbers!

Ken: That's good. I'm trying to keep my expenses down this month.

Megan: So am I. I expect tonight'll cost about $20.

Ken: You must be good with money. I expect it to come to ... um ... nearly $40! So how are you going to manage that?

Megan: Well, the bus is cheap, and if I come home early I won't have time to spend too much! In any case, I have to be up early tomorrow morning, so I'd really better try to get home by about 11.

Ken: That reminds me. I have to phone the taxi company for my mother. Goodbye, Megan. I'll see you later.

Megan: Goodbye, Ken.

Sound of phone hanging up.

Narrator: Ken calls the taxi company. Listen and be ready to answer questions 8 and 9. Now listen to the telephone call and be ready to answer questions 8 and 9.

Sound of somebody dialling, phone ringing

Man's voice: Hello, this is Acme Cabs. Please follow the instructions on the tape.

If you wish to order a cab now, press 1.

If you have placed an order previously, press 2.

If you wish to make an advance order, Press 3. Please be ready to tell us your street number and name.

If you wish to speak to the radio room supervisor, press 4.

If you want to enquire about lost property, press 5.

If you want to order a taxi equipped to carry wheelchairs, press 6.

Your call is very important. Please stay on the line for the next available order taker.

Click to indicate a real person is there.

Ken: Hello. I think I left something in one of your cabs on Thursday. It was a brown paper package with an address written on it in green ink. Has anyone handed it in?

Narrator: That is the end of Section 1. You now have some time to check your answers.

Now turn to Section 2.

Section 2. You are going to hear some announcements made to a group of people who are planning a trip to Greece. First look at questions 10 to 15. As you listen to the first part of the talk answer questions 10 to 15. Write no more than three words or numbers for each answer.

Tour organiser: Good morning everyone. I'm getting very excited about this trip to Greece, and I'm sure you are too. As you know, we didn't have all the details at our last meeting, but I can give them to you now. We'll leave London Gatwick Airport on British Airways next Wednesday. Please be sure to be at the airport by 6.30. I know it's early, but our departure time is 8.25 AM. We're quite a large group, and we don't want to have any hassles. Please be sure to have all your travel documents ready. We'll arrive in Athens at 2.25 in the afternoon, and there'll be a vehicle there to meet us. It'll be a full sized coach so everyone can travel together.

We'll spend three full days in our hotel in Athens, although we're only being charged for two nights' accommodation, which is good news. The second day we'll go to the National Archaeological Museum to see the enormous collection of ancient Greek works of art, antiques, statues – a brilliant display. We'll eat out at a typical Greek restaurant on Thursday night. It's going to be a very busy time in Athens! Friday morning and afternoon we'll visit historic sites, but we have nothing planned for the rest of the day. On Saturday we're off to the islands, the Greek islands of ancient myth and modern romance. Now, the big

THE NEW PREPARE FOR IELTS: Academic Modules

Unit 6 Answers and tapescripts

news! At first we thought we'd take the ferry, but we've been very lucky to secure a sailing boat which is big enough for all of us. I'm really excited about this part of the trip, because we'll see the islands to the best advantage, and we'll be able to cruise around and sleep on board. We'll get off at different islands and for one part of the trip we'll have people playing Greek traditional music actually on board with us. Now I'll pass out a brochure with all the details.

Narrator: Now look at questions 16 to 18. As the talk continues answer questions 16 to 18.

Tour organiser: A lot of work has gone into organising this tour, and I'd like to thank in particular the travel agent who got us a really good deal and the people at the British Museum who offered us such good advice. Trips like this only happen because of the hard work of really expert people.

As you know, we have planned a gathering for when we return. I have a list of things which the committee would like you to bring to the party. They are: your pictures and something to eat for everyone to share. You are almost bound to have people ask what we have in common, and why we are travelling as a group. I suppose the answer is that we are interested in learning about old societies and vanished cultures, and we all enjoy travelling. Of course, we enjoy fine food too, but that's not as important!

Narrator: Now look at questions 19 and 20. As the talk continues answer questions 19 and 20.

Tour organiser: I nearly forgot the last piece of information. You will see there are labels which I have passed around for you to put on all your luggage. Could you fill them in, please? On the top line please write "Greek tour" and on the lower line, write, in block letters, I mean upper case, the letters AA and the number 3 - that's AA3.

We need to have these labels clearly displayed to help the baggage handlers keep our luggage together on the different parts of our trip, so please don't take them off.

Narrator: That is the end of section 2. You now have some time to check your answers. Now turn to section 3.

Section 3. You are going to hear Dr Joanne Robinson, the course director of a Language Learning Center, answering questions from reporters from the student newspaper. First look at questions 21 to 26. As you listen to the first part of the talk, answer questions 21 to 26. Write no more than three words or numbers for each answer.

Course Director: Welcome to the Language Learning Center. I'm Joanne Robinson. You must be the reporters from *The Examiner*. Please come in and sit down.

Cheryl: Hello Dr Robinson. Yes, we're from *The Examiner*. I'm Cheryl Perkins and this is Don Klim. May I start with a question? Did this college really start with Brazilian students?

Course Director: It did. The Language Learning Center was founded in 1985 to look after a group of students from Brazil who wanted to study here. Those twenty students soon grew to 60, and, as you

can imagine, we had severe accommodation problems.

Don: Somebody said you were in the old amenities block, right near the engineering school.

Course Director: They have a good memory! Yes, we were there, because the university hadn't believed we would expand so quickly. The problem wasn't solved until we moved into these new premises in Bancroft House in 1987.

Don: When did you start taking students from other countries?

Course Director: About 1990. We now have students from 13 different countries enrolled, and we expect a large group from Turkey next month.

Cheryl: Yes, we've noticed a lot more advertisements for Turkish restaurants in our advertising section.

Course Director: Well, 40% of our students come from Turkey, by far the largest single national group, and I believe there's been an influx to the rest of the university. There are a lot of Turkish students studying hospitality.

Cheryl: Do you offer anything special to the students?

Course Director: Yes, we do. There are several things which make us rather different from other language schools. English is certainly not restricted to English for academic purposes here! Sometimes we have extra classes for students who have particular courses in mind, and we have just said goodbye to a group of thirty Indonesian students who were preparing for a university course in agriculture. They came to us for English for farming, and they were with us for a long time. We miss them!

Cheryl: How long do students usually stay at the Language Learning Center?

Course Director: It varies, so I'll talk about the average. Most of our courses last for five weeks, but to make any real progress a student needs to be here for at least three terms, that's fifteen weeks. The students do better if they have a little time to settle in at the beginning of the course, and we offer an orientation course that lasts a week. Most students take it. It helps them to settle down, and it gives us plenty of time to test them and place them at the right level.

Don: How many people are in each class?

Course Director: We sometimes go up to 18, but our average class size is 14 students, and some classes have as few as seven participants. It depends on the needs of the group.

Cheryl: You were saying that you miss your students when they go. How do you attract students? I mean, how do they hear about the Language Learning Center in the first place?

Course Director: We're included in the university advertising and marketing, and we have our own website. The thing which works best for us, though, is word of mouth. Students who leave us often send us their friends. In fact, a student who arrived today was carrying a photograph for me of a former student and his baby!

Cheryl: It sounds like a nice place to be!

Course Director: It is! A lot of our students make lasting friendships while they're here.

Narrator: Now look at questions 27 to 31. As the talk continues, answer questions 27 to 31.

Cheryl: Making friends with other students sounds special enough! I'd like to emphasise that in the student newspaper.

Course Director: We do try to get our students to be part of the wider university.

Don: How do you do that? Do you encourage them to join the Sports Center, for instance?

Course Director: Indeed we do! The Sports Center is always looking for active participants, particularly in soccer. Oh, and something else. You might like to mention that we don't teach just English here. I mean, we're a language center, not an English language center. You may learn Spanish, Mandarin, and Russian here, and we can sometimes offer other languages. This means we can have some students who are native speakers of those languages as conversation partners for English-speaking students.

Cheryl: Who can do those courses?

Course Director: At this time, any native speaker of English.

Cheryl: What about the people who are learning English? Can they do a non-English language course?

Course Director: At this time, only if they've almost finished their English language course. You see, we try very hard to involve students who are native speakers of English as conversation leaders and we encourage our students to join groups on the campus. For instance, if they enjoy music, there is an active jazz group available to everyone, and that's a lot of fun. On the other hand, elementary students can't go to the drama group, their English just isn't ready for that sort of activity, but the university choir welcomes all the singers it can find. They often do large productions that need a lot of voices.

Cheryl: I imagine the special conversation groups are open to all your students …

Course Director: I wish they were. I'm sorry to say they're a special service we provide for elementary students only. Is there anything else I can tell you? *(pause)* I'd be really pleased if you could write about the courses we offer in foreign languages.

Cheryl: I think our readers would be very interested in that. Thank you for your time, Dr Robinson.

Don: Yes, thank you very much.

Course Director: Goodbye. Thank you for giving me the opportunity to talk about the center. It's always good to let the rest of the students at the university know what goes on in our classrooms, and outside them! After all, many of our students leave us and then study for degrees in various disciplines on this campus.

Narrator: That is the end of Section 3. You will now have some time to check your answers. Now turn to Section 4

Section 4 You will hear a talk about the pitfalls and pleasures of being a postgraduate student.

Look at questions 32 to 37. Listen to the speaker's advice and answer questions 32 to 37. Circle the correct letter.

Speaker: Postgraduates are about as easy to define as catching steam in a bucket. Courses can be vocational, for training, as research, as a preparation for research, or a combination of these. Also you can choose between full-time and part-time. Increasingly, the approach to postgraduate study is becoming modular. The vast majority of postgraduates are doing short, taught courses, many of which provide specific vocational training. Indeed, there has been a 400% increase in postgraduate numbers in Britain over the past 20 years. Current figures stand at just under 400,000.

People undertake postgraduate study for many reasons. These may be academic (intellectual challenge, development of knowledge), vocational (training for a specific career goal) or only vague (drifting into further study). It is essential that you determine the reasons you want to become a postgraduate. If you have clear goals and reasons for studying, this will enhance your learning experience and help you to remain focused and motivated throughout your course.

Where you study should be based on much more than the course you want to do. For some courses you are likely to be there for several years, and it is important that you are happy living there. Check also what type of accommodation is available and whether the institution provides any housing specifically for postgraduates.

Choosing an institution and department is a difficult process. To determine quality, do not rely on the reputation of an institution, but find out what ratings are from the most recent assessment exercises. Find out about the staff, their reputation, competence, enthusiasm and friendliness. Visit the department if possible and talk to existing postgraduates about their experience, satisfaction, comments and complaints. Be very careful to check how they feel about their supervisors.

Also, check what facilities are available, both at an institutional level (for example libraries, laboratory and computing facilities) and in the department (for example study room, desk, photocopying, secretarial support etc). Everyone will have their own priorities here: I am always anxious to check the computer support available, and regard it as slightly more important than library access. Your working environment and the support available to you plays an essential part in making your work as a postgraduate a positive experience.

Life as a postgraduate can be very different to your other experiences of education. Things that can distinguish your experience are the level of study, independence of working, intensity of the course, the demands on your time, and often the fact that you are older than the majority of the students.

These factors can contribute to making you feel isolated. However, there are several ways you can make sure that this is either short-lived or does not happen at all.

Many student unions have postgraduate societies that organise social events and may also provide representation for postgraduates to both the student union and the institution. Departments can also help to create a sense of identity and community, and often have discussion groups available. Don't be afraid to talk to staff about any difficulties you might be having. Of course universities provide counselling services but we have found that the best advice comes from talking to other postgraduates who may have faced similar difficulties.

Narrator: Look at questions 38 to 40. Write no more than three words or numbers for each answer.

Speaker: Financial planning is essential, since the government excludes postgraduates from student loans, and it can be difficult to maintain your student status with banks. This has implications for free banking and overdraft facilities. Do not underestimate your living costs, including food, accommodation and travel, and be careful not to budget for everything except a social life.

Funding a course is one of the most challenging things people face when considering postgraduate study. Most postgraduate students are self-financing. They pay (often very large) fees to the institution and receive no maintenance income to support their study.

Make sure you know exactly what your costs will be - institutions often hide extra fees like laboratory costs behind the headline fee rate advertised.

Funding can come from various sources. Research councils, charities, trust funds, institutional scholarships, local education authorities and professional bodies and organisations all offer various levels of funding. As I said before, the government excludes postgraduates from student loans, so it is essential you look to other sources. Career development loans are available from high street banks. The best advice on funding is to be proactive, persistent and patient.

The postgraduate community in Britain is multinational, has a wide range of experience of life and work and an exciting mix of goals, both career and academic. Being a postgraduate student should be a productive and fulfilling thing to do, and you will become part of a diverse and motivated social group.

Narrator: That is the end of Section 4. You now have some time to check your answers.

That is the end of Listening Practice Test 5.

Part 2: Academic Reading Practice Tests

Answer Key: Academic Reading Practice Test 1

Reading Passage 1:   Airconditioning the Earth

1. 10,000 kilometres	5. polar regions	9. P	13. B
2. 10 kilometres	6. latitude	10. P	
3. convection cells	7. at sea	11. U	
4. equatorial regions	8. N	12. C	

Reading Passage 2:   Money as the Unit of Account

14. ii	18. E	22. A	26. A
15. vi	19. G	23. B	
16. iii	20. I	24. A	
17. iv	21. C	25. C	

Reading Passage 3:   Refining Petroleum

27. light hydrocarbons	32. catalyst in powder	37. primary distillation
28. (a) kerosene (fraction)	33. catalyst separated out	38. heavy distillates / heavier
29. (light) fuel-oil distillate	34. catalyst purified	distillates
30. catalytic cracking	35. boiling range	39. atmospheric
31. catalyst in pellets	36. separate	40. 20 to 30

Answer Key: Academic Reading Practice Test 2

Reading Passage 1:   Jupiter's Bruises

1. YES
2. NO
3. NOT GIVEN
4. NO (the whole passage indicates that he was taken seriously)
5. NO
6. NO
7. YES
8. Hubble Space Telescope
9. carbon monoxide
10. water and oxygen
11. colour
12. cyclone / Great Red Spot

Reading Passage 2:   Fashion and Society

13. B
14. D
15. & 16.   nuns, the poor, hippies (order not important, but must have two)
17. & 18.   a pink suit, a skirt (order not important)
19. G
20. E
21. B
22. D
23. C
24. F
25. D
26. G

Reading Passage 3:   Mass Production

27. 1903
28. 1908
29. 1913
30. early 1920s
31. D
32. B
33. A
34. C
35. NG
36. D
37. A
38. A
39. D
40. B
41. A
42. C

Answer Key: Academic Reading Practice Test 3

Reading Passage 1:   Myths about Public Speaking

1. B
2. C
3. A
4. D
5. C
6. NO
7. YES
8. NOT GIVEN
9. NOT GIVEN
10. YES
11. NO
12. stimulation
13. 60%
14. poor listening habits

Reading Passage 2:   Environmental Effects of Offshore Drilling and Production

15. D
16. B
17. C
18. 10 kl / 63 barrels
19. 6
20. Platform oil spills
21. SK-2
22. DW
23. SK-1
24. DO
25. C
26. PW
27. DW
28. PW

Reading Passage 3:   Garbage In, Garbage Out

29. Tucson
30. Mexico
31. standardised coding form
32. census
33. principles
34. methodology
35. landfills
36. A
37. B
38. A
39. A
40. A & F (must have both)
41. D & K (must have both)
42. J & L (must have both)

Answer Key: Academic Reading Practice Test 4

Reading Passage 1:   Hazardous Compounds Help to Preserve Crumbling Books

1. NO	5. A ⎤	9. L	13. F
2. YES	6. C ⎬ in any order	10. G	14. C
3. YES	7. E	11. I	15. K
4. NG	8. F ⎦	12. B	16. C

Reading Passage 2:   Drugs and Obesity

17. D	21. G	25. C	29. L
18. C	22. E	26. H	30. I
19. C	23. D	27. F	31. K
20. A	24. H	28. B	

Reading Passage 3:   The Introduction of the Aged Pension in Australia

32. 3.4%/per cent	35. £310	38. Universalism	41. Liberal
33. 1891	36. £26	39. Sydney Maxted	individualism
34. 1901	37. £52	40. E. W. O'Sullivan	42. Universalism

Answer Key: Academic Reading Practice Test 5

Reading passage 1:   The Dams that Changed Australia

1. vi	4. iv	7. 1973	10. YES
2. vii	5. 1788	8. reunion	11. NOT GIVEN
3. i	6. 1949	9. NO	12. YES

Reading Passage 2:   Power from the Earth

13. E	17. B	21. YES	25. NO
14. H	18. G	22. NOT GIVEN	26. NOT GIVEN
15. D	19. NO	23. YES	
16. C	20. NOT GIVEN	24. YES	

Reading Passage 3:   Are we Managing to Destroy Science?

27. conducted	31. strict	35. YES	39. NOT GIVEN
28. worried	32. publish	36. NOT GIVEN	40. YES
29. rated	33. expensive	37. NO	
30. academic/scientific	34. replace	38. YES	

Part 3: Academic Writing Practice Tests - Suggestions

Academic Writing Practice Test 1
Task 1 The answer should describe the information in the two graphs and show the similarities and differences between them. Describe the changes: what is more, what is less and what is the same.

Task 2 The answer should describe some of the different ways people feel about medical treatment. Say if in your opinion the feelings affect the treatment or not. Give examples to support your argument.

Academic Writing Practice Test 2
Task 1 The answer should describe how nitrogen gets into and is taken out of the groundwater.

Task 2 The answer should explain what you think a government should do. Give reasons for your opinion, with examples to show why your opinion is right. Give reasons and examples to show why other opinions are not right.

Academic Writing Practice Test 3
Task 1 The answer should discuss the information in each graph. Describe which employment areas employ the most people and how each area contributes to GDP. Describe how these factors change over time.

Task 2 The answer should consider each of the three related questions. Show which subjects can benefit from the use of a computer. Show what cannot be taught by computer, and explain why a computer cannot help in these areas. The conclusion should show whether you believe computers are essential in education or not, using arguments from your essay.

Academic Writing Practice Test 4
Task 1 The answer should discuss the information on the table. Describe the results for each country and each feature.

Task 2 The answer should suggest some ways to stop people from using their cars so much, e.g. government measures, education campaigns.

Academic Writing Practice Test 5
Task 1 The answer should recognise that the graphs are on two different scales, and should compare the two groups in terms of trends and absolute numbers.

Task 2 The answer should give reasons for either educating people broadly or for specific tasks, and end with a conclusion where the writer states which system he/she prefers.

Acknowledgements

Sources of texts:

"Postgraduate Courses - pitfalls and pleasures of being a postgraduate", by Jeremy Hoad, from *The Guardian Weekly*, 7 June 2000, used with the permission of *The Guardian* London; first published in *The Guardian*.

"Airconditioning the Earth", reprinted with permission from *Geographia Atlas of the World*, 1984, © Esselte Map Service, Stockholm amd Geographia Ltd UK.

"Money as the unit of account", reprinted with permission from *Honest Money*, N. R. Evans and Kevin Dowd, © Australian Institute for Public Policy, Policy Paper No. 21, 1992.

"Refining Petroleum", reprinted with permission of the publisher from "Petroleum", by Frank M. Clagett, *Collier's Encyclopedia*, Vol. 18, pp. 628-652. Copyright © 1995 by P. F. Collier, L. P.

"Jupiter's Bruises", reprinted with permission from *Time*, August 1, 1994, pp. 52-53, © Time/Life Syndication.

"Fashion and Society", written by Vanessa Todd, © Insearch Language Centre, 1996.

"Mass Production", reprinted with permission of Rawson Associates/Scribner, an imprint of Simon & Schuster from *The Machine that Changed the World* by James P. Womack, Daniel T. Jones, Daniel Roos. Copyright © 1990 James P. Womack, Daniel T. Jones, Daniel Roos and Donna Sammons Carpenter.

"Myths about Public Speaking", reprinted with permission of the author, from Professionally Speaking, © Robert J. Doolittle, Scott, Foresman & Co., 1984.

"Environmental Effects of Offshore Drilling and Production", reprinted with permission from "Oil in Troubled Waters", P. Purcell, *Environmental Backgrounder*, No. 15, July 1993, © Institute of Public Affairs, West Perth.

"Garbage In, Garbage Out", reprinted with permission from "Down to earth", Ron Brunton, *IPA Review*, 46:1, 1993, © Institute of Public Affairs, Jolimont.

"Hazardous compound helps to preserve crumbling books", reprinted with permission from *New Scientist*, 18 November 1989, © Reed Business Publishing.

"Drugs and Obesity", written by Vanessa Todd, © Insearch Language Centre, 1996.

"The introduction of the aged pension in Australia", reprinted with permission from *No Charity There*, Brian Dickey, © Allen & Unwin, Sydney, 1987.

"On the home front: Power from the Earth" used with the permission of the editor of Pacific Friend Volume 2000, Number 4, pp. 5-7.

"Are we Managing to Stifle Science?", by Michael J Larkin, Chemistry and Industry, 21 June 1999, p. 488 used with the permission of the editor.

"Post-School Qualifications", reprinted with permission from *Education Monitor*, Spring 1991, No. 4. © Institute of Public Affairs, Jolimont.

"Nitrogen cycle in groundwater", reprinted with permission from *The West Australian*, July 7, 1995, p. 10, © West Australian Newspapers Limited.

"Consumer preferences as to automatic washing machines", reprinted with permission from "The Globalization of Markets", *Harvard Business Review*, May/June 1983, © 1983 by the President and Fellows of Harvard College.

New Scientist magazine, the weekly review of science and technology, provides an outstanding source of articles for comprehensive exercises. *New Scientist* is a most useful and accessible magazine for this purpose. For subscriptions to *New Scientist*, write to the Circulation Department, PO Box 5487, West Chatswood NSW 2057, Australia or fax 61 2 9412 3317.

The producers of this book would like to thank the staff of Insearch, University of Technology, Sydney and of Sydney Institute of Technology Ultimo Campus, who have willingly trialled the materials and generously given their time and opinions. Their assistance, expertise, support and encouragement were greatly appreciated and made this project possible. To the students of Insearch go our thanks for their cheerful willingness to work through more practice tests than they would ever want to face in reality, and for their very useful comments on the contents.

The audio cassettes owe much to the technical skill of Allan Black of Black Inc Recorders Pty Ltd and to the voices of Jean Brennan, Sharon Brigden, Tim Connors, Kate Delaney, Ann-Maree Dombroski, Peter Doyle, Gwynedd Duncan-Jones, Quentin Fuller, Philip Godber, Audrey Low, Annie Marlow, Robert Nash, Adrian Norman and Sharon Sinnes.

The author's special thanks for help with the new edition go to Erik Johansen.